Also by L. E. Hewitt

Life Between the Raindrops
My Wonderful Chaos
Chasing the Silver Lining
My Bucket List Has a Hole in It
I Don't Have A Button for That

Free TP
and
Frog Cures

L.E. HEWITT

SEABOARD PRESS

JAMES A. ROCK & COMPANY, PUBLISHERS

Free TP and Frog Cures by L. E. Hewitt

SEABOARD PRESS

is an imprint of JAMES A. ROCK & CO., PUBLISHERS

Free TP and Frog Cures copyright ©2017 by L.E. Hewitt

Special contents of this edition copyright ©2017 by Seaboard Press

Address comments and inquiries to:
SEABOARD PRESS
1937 West Palmetto Street, #248
Florence, South Carolina 29501

E-mail:
jarrock@sprintmail.com   lar-rock@earthlink.net
Internet URL: www.rockpublishing.com

Trade Paperback ISBN: 978-1-59663-882-2

Printed in the United States of America

First Edition: 2017

*Interested readers may
wish to visit the author's website:*

www.lehewitt.net

*Dedicated to
the memory of
my parents*

Betty and Fred

*They raised me
well*

Contents

Foreword

I have found that there is never a point in my life where I can look forward and predict, with any sort of accuracy, what will happen in the future. I have tried. I've always been wrong. Often, something even better than I expected has happened. I do choose to embrace the good things. I choose to celebrate my being here. I experience this life in my own unique way.

Observing the way children observe the world has been a great inspiration to me. They tend to see the little details that we adults often miss. This is where I often find the subjects for my stories, the little stuff. The world is in a constant state of change all around us. Try not to be blind to these things, as they are often beautiful.

My hope for this book, as with the previous five, is to make you laugh a lot, cry a little, and to reflect upon your own life with, hopefully, a smile. The stories you are about to encounter are based on true stories from my own life and the lives of those around me. Also, there is an expansion to my subject matter this time around. I attempted a couple of social experiments. First of all, I selected random people out of the crowd and asked them if I could interview them. I promised to never reveal their identity, and in return, they promised to tell me their whole, true story. It was an amazing experience that I will never forget.

My second project was to become a ride-share driver part time for a few months, so that I could share the stories of the people

I encountered. It is amazing what you can learn about someone during a fifteen minute car ride together. This adventure was highly entertaining. There is a whole different world out there at 3AM on a Saturday night!

I do hope you enjoy reading this book. I know I certainly enjoy the love my readers have shown me in return over the years.

More Wine?

My ridesharing experiment is very early in its existence, yet I may never experience another story quite like the one that I am about to share with you. I am meeting all sorts of interesting people and having a great time talking and listening. Probably more often than not, I am picking up a group of two, three or even four. In those cases, I only join the conversation when invited, choosing instead to be that fly on the wall. I find that most of my passengers do not hold back just because I am a stranger in their midst. I typically get to hear the whole story and to enjoy the free entertainment. Actually, it is beyond free, because I am getting paid to drive while I listen! It's a win-win.

Probably 95% of my customers are professional, middle-class individuals. You get a few on either end of the economic spectrum, but predominately, these are successful, yet hard-working people. This case is no exception. It was late and I was on my way home, within a mile of my house. My phone dinged. I had yet another ride request. I could have just declined it and headed on home. I had already driven countless riders. I was tired. It was late. But, I figured, what the heck, this one was only about six blocks away. So, I accepted.

I arrived at a private residence in this middle-class neighborhood. I pulled in the driveway. A nicely dressed, harmless looking forty-year-old man came out the door leading an obviously intoxicated, professionally dressed woman of about the same age toward my car. He opened the door and inserted the woman into my back seat and told her that I was her driver who would be taking her home. He confirmed with me that I had received the destination address. Then he closed her door and smiled and waved as we drove away.

The woman seemed pleasant enough. She engaged in small talk. She had been to a company party put on by her employer. They had filet mignon for dinner and they had been dancing to a deejay.

The conversation waned a bit until a couple of minutes later when she spoke up and asked, "Who are you and where are you taking me?"

"I am your driver and I am taking you home" I replied.

"Oh, okay," she replied. "Do you want to come in for a drink when we get there?"

"No, I am sorry" I responded, "I am working and you have already had too much to drink." I was trying to be polite and respectful.

Once again she grew quiet. She appeared to drift off to sleep a bit. This was a twenty-mile trip, so I was a bit thankful.

Maybe ten minutes later she once again returned to consciousness. Once again she asked, "Who are you and where are you taking me?"

Once again I responded, "I am your driver and I am taking you home," as I looked at her in my rear view mirror.

My passenger started to say something else, but instead, the next sensation I felt was warm red wine laced with bits of steak and some sort of fruit salad running down the back of my head and neck. My passenger, my car, and I were all now covered in foul smelling vomit with another five miles to go to her house. I pulled over and dragged out a roll of paper towels from the trunk. This lady was so embarrassed. I could tell she just wanted to crawl in a hole somewhere and at that point I was probably willing to help her. I wiped down the car and myself as best that I could and I gave her a supply of towels to do the same. There was then nothing left to do but to finish this journey. She had once again become quiet.

My passenger remained asleep the remainder of the drive. The only thing coming from her was a strong repulsive odor of rotten grapes and alcohol. When we arrived in her driveway, I spoke to her to awaken her.

"Oh, we are home!" she said as she seemed to perk up a bit, "Are you gonna come in for a drink?"

"Uh, no. I think I have had plenty of wine for one evening, thank you." I responded.

She then popped out of the car and staggered to her front door. Me, I rolled down all of the windows and drove home looking like a dog on a summer car ride, my head hanging out of the window the whole way.

Estelle

At 44, Estelle appeared petite and timid. She had a warm smile and my initial impression was of someone who could not hurt a soul. She had a bit of a haunted look of fear in her eyes. Something hidden, perhaps a hole in her emotional heart. I knew that she was happily married and had a good home but I wondered what was behind those eyes.

"I am in a good place in my life right now. Sure, I worry about things like bills and my husband's job, but I go to the gym multiple times a week to do exercise classes like aerobics and zumba. I have made several friends there. I have a good relationship with my father now. That wasn't always true, but I have been able to form my own opinions about him. I also do well with my husband's family. With them, I was afraid at first as to whether they would accept me, but they have been very good to me. My health issues are improved. My service dog has been a lifesaver," Estelle began.

I learned that Estelle suffers from severe anxiety and major depression. The service dog was in her life to provide comfort and balance and had been a lifesaving addition for the past five years.

It was not the 'typical' use for a service animal as we more often see them for deaf and blind folks, but it was just what the doctor ordered for her. This, in combination with electroconvulsive therapy, had made her life an easier place to be. Estelle explained the therapy to me. Basically, once every three weeks she goes and is anesthetized. Electrodes are then attached to her head and a monitored series of shocks are applied to her brain to shock it into having a small seizure. The purpose is to trick the brain into releasing chemicals that help to combat her anxiety and depression. This was a sort of last resort effort after all known medicines had failed to produce desired results.

"Prior to finding this treatment, things were ugly. I would mentally try to write the book before events happened. My poor husband would come home to find me hysterical, holding a knife, telling him that I just couldn't take it anymore. I never actually attempted suicide, but the thought was present," Estelle revealed. "My husband was scared that he would come home one day and find me dead. He stuck right with me through the worst of times."

Things had not always been this way for Estelle. She entered college on a scholarship as a promising ballerina. She went to one school and then transferred on another scholarship to a second school that held promise for her budding career. She talked about how she loved performing for a crowd and had a passion for her dancing. Eventually, she did give up her dancing and transferred home to be closer to her future husband. She ended up earning her degree in business. She then worked in her career field for about five years during which time her anxiety and depression symptoms appeared and worsened to the point they became disabling.

"Where did this depression come from?" I asked.

"Well, it probably is rooted in the fact that I was abused as a child. My mother and father divorced when I was four-years-old. My older sister and I were raised predominately by my mother. I was told that my father was an evil man and so I grew up believing that to be true. I tried so hard to fit in, to be accepted. My mother always badmouthed me and told me that my being born was a mistake," Estelle recalled. "I think that maybe it was because I looked so much like my dad, but I was never accepted by my mom the way my sister was. I really never fit in. I felt like such an outcast. I would say something wrong and not even understand what I had done and my mom would lock me in the closet, sometimes for days at a time. No food, no water, no bathroom. I was so scared, so sad. I just had to do what I had to do to survive."

"I tried and tried to fit in. I didn't understand. My sister and mother were always close. I just wanted to be a part. In the end they actually disowned me on Christmas day nineteen years ago. They were upset because they felt I had not spent enough on their gifts. I was poor and struggling financially but they didn't care. They called me an ungrateful, selfish bitch. They still live in the same area and I often wonder what they are up to. I just wanted to fix everything, but I had to let go of that and accept things as they are." Estelle sighed. "The good thing that came out of this was that I got the chance to know my father for the man that he truly is. We have a very good relationship now."

"I didn't go to church growing up, but now I go every Sunday. I am not afraid to die. I just don't want to die alone. I want to go before my husband so that I don't ever have to be alone. Now that things are improved for me, I want to socialize more and travel more. I have a lot of life ahead of me."

The End

She was standing in front of a nice house in a middle-class neighborhood holding a suitcase when I arrived. She put her luggage in the back seat and asked if it was okay if she sat up front with me. I, of course, had no objections and actually preferred it. I always enjoy being able to see the person I am talking to without using the mirror. She told me that she assumed that I could tell that she was headed for the airport.

Her name was Katie. She was probably in her forties, an attractive, slender blonde, with her medium length hair cropped close to her face. It was a warm, friendly face. Sometimes you just have a gut feeling about these things. I asked her the normal question about how her day was going and she said it was okay. She asked me the normal question about how I liked doing rideshares. I told her I loved it. I told her that I had met lots of interesting people and had many funny stories to tell from my experience so far.

"Well, I could certainly use a funny story today!" she pronounced.

I proceeded to tell Katie about the passenger who called people at 3am because she was feeling old, and I also shared the experience of the woman who kept waking up and asking me who I was and where I was taking her. I then revealed that I was doing ridesharing so that I could write a book about all the fascinating people that I meet.

"Well, I suppose that I should share with you my story then, shouldn't I?" she said with a halfway smile. "The house where you picked me up belongs to a man I met during a tropical vacation about nine months ago. We fell very hard for each other. My job allows for flexibility in location, so I have been coming here and staying a week at a time on a frequent basis."

"And where is home?" I asked.

"Texas." Katie answered.

"Well, I am a transplant from Pennsylvania." I pronounced proudly.

"Tell me, is everyone here … how should I put this? Does everyone here talk with such … animation?" she queried.

"Animation?" I probed.

"Yes, um, all of his friends, especially the female ones, well they act so … out there. Each time they see me that are like 'Oh, we are so happy to see you!' over the top. Reminds me of the women on that TV show, The Bachelor. Are all people like that around here?" she asked.

"Um, no." I said with a chuckle. "Sounds like it's just the type of crowd he runs with. Most people here are very conservative, down to earth folks."

"Good to know." she said as she appeared to be absorbing my perspective. "He owns a business and his passion is being on the water on weekends. We spent lots of time out on a boat last summer.

Katie paused a moment before continuing, "Today is probably the last time I will be here. We had a disagreement last night. He just has some maturity issues. He keeps saying things will get better once this happens or that happens, but I am not really seeing the changes."

"Are you sure it's over?" I probed.

"Well, it's 12:30 and my flight isn't until 6:00," she confessed. "But you are looking for positive or funny stories for your book. Let me tell you one!"

I could see that Katie needed a diversion from the gloomy situation she was in, so I listened intently.

"I went to Europe and hitchhiked my way around the continent when I was younger. I didn't have much money, but there were places that I wanted to see. I did what I could to be careful and I gained an appreciation for truckers. My most memorable moment occurred while riding with a trucker across northern France. He didn't know English and I didn't know French. We were in a very rural area when we came upon a primitive rest stop. It was not much more than a wide spot in the road with picnic tables. He pulled over the truck. Needless to say, I was concerned. I braced myself in preparation for a fight or to jump out and run away if need be. The driver motioned me to get out of the truck. I refused and made it clear that I was perfectly fine staying right where I was! He was insistent. He motioned that he wanted me to come with him back to the trailer he was towing. I responded firmly, no! Finally, he relented and went back to the trailer alone. He soon returned with some lettuce and strawberries and handed them to me. Well, now he was talking food! Now, I was happy to get out of the truck! He had simply wanted to feed me from the load of produce he was hauling!"

Katie's mood was lightening. We talked about books and places we wanted to travel and about life. We had become unlikely buddies during a forty-minute journey. As we neared the airport, I told her to stick to her guns because, as we both knew, it was likely that this man she was leaving would promise to make changes to his life, but those changes usually turn out to only be temporary.

Then she said, "That's enough about him! I am just gonna stay mad at him for now! I can't break down and cry until I get home."

With that, we quietly enjoyed the last little portion of our journey together. It had been a very memorable encounter. When we reached the terminal, we said our goodbyes and I wished her luck, as she did me. I will always wonder and probably never know how her love story actually ends, but I am glad that I got to take that journey with her and share the moment so that I could share it with you.

Floppy

This is the story of Floppy the Duck as was shared with me by an old friend.

"My brother won Floppy when he was a baby duck as a prize at a community Easter Egg Hunt," Janice said. "It was late March and still chilly outside, so he got to live in the house until warmer weather came. Mom would let him swim in the kitchen sink and then as he grew, his swimming location was moved to the bathroom tub."

As the weather warmed, Floppy was transferred to the outside where he had the run of his new country location. Floppy turned out to have a mean streak. He would attack anyone but Janice's mom. They never figured out what he was so mad about. Nobody ever mistreated him. They even got him two girl ducks to keep him company. He seemed to like the girl ducks, but he still had this thing against humans.

"He would be nice if you had something good to feed him, but other than that, forget it!" Janine lamented. "Before exiting the house, you always had to do a scouting exercise out the windows in order to pinpoint Floppy's location. Then, at the right moment, you would make a mad dash for the car before he caught you and made you pay with a severe pecking! One time my poor brother wrecked his bicycle in the yard. As he was lying there, before anyone was aware of his predicament, Floppy came along and gave him a good pecking around the face and neck."

Some of the more entertaining events would occur when unexpected visitors would arrive at Janice's house.

"We would usually be alerted by their screams as they ran around the yard trying to escape Floppy's onslaught," Janice laughed. "We didn't need a guard dog. We had our very own attack duck! He had quite a bad reputation and he was a fixture at our place for years"

Floppy actually ended up living a long and happy life hanging out with his duck buddies and chasing humans. You could honestly say that he 'left his mark' on the world he lived in.

Drop That Car

It was 11:30 pm on New Year's Eve. Why in the world would I be doing ridesharing at this time? Well, I basically live alone. Will still comes home during college breaks, but hanging out with dad on New Years Eve was not his idea of a great way to spend the holiday. Besides, I thought it could be a great night to pick up a story or two. So, I found myself in downtown Indianapolis, thirty minutes away from the big moment that everyone was waiting for. My phone beeped. I had a ride request just a few minutes from my current position. Along with an address, I was provided with a first name of the rider I was to pick up, Mei-Xing. Within five minutes, I was at her apartment and she was entering my car.

"Hello sir, I need to go downtown to the festival," she offered, "down to near the Fieldhouse."

The Fieldhouse is where the professional basketball teams of the NBA and WNBA play. This was right in the middle of an area blocked off for a New Years Eve street festival. I explained to my passenger that I could only get her within a few blocks due to street closings in that area. She acknowledged that she understood.

"I am here in the United States for one year." Mei-Xing continued. "I am here for my studies. I was downtown to the festival earlier because I wanted to see how American culture celebrates your new year. Chinese New Year is a very big holiday. Since I am only here for one year, this was my only chance to see what is different here. I left the festival about 8:30 but I got home and realized that I have lost my car keys. I am going back to find them."

My heart sank. This poor young woman was going to an area of a few square blocks filled with a few thousand people to look for a set of keys. Her only real hope was that perhaps she had lost them in a restaurant where she had eaten. But, she was determined to at least try.

This was the first year for this particular celebration. Someone had gotten the idea that since Times Square has the big ball that they drop at midnight, that Indianapolis should drop something too. An Indy Racecar! Yep, that's right. They hoisted an Indy Racecar high into the air with a crane, to be dropped from the sky at midnight onto the middle of Pennsylvania Street.

As Mei-Xing and I drove, we chatted about America and China and missing family and food. We were weaving our way through traffic. My goal was to get her down Pennsylvania Street as far as I could until we came to the barricades. As fate would have it, we arrived at our desired location at the perfect time. Just as we reached the end of the road, straight ahead we could see the racecar. It was beginning its descent. They had attached flashing lights to it for effect and the moment that it touched the ground, fireworks erupted. I have spent many New Years Eves in many different ways, but this was the first time that I got to share it in a car with a total stranger from China. I did not disclose to her the American custom of kissing the person that you are with at midnight. The poor girl already had enough things to worry about! As we ended our journey together, we both chuckled at the thought of how unlikely it was that we had shared such a moment. I wished her luck and she was on her way, quickly disappearing into the crowd. I knew that our paths would probably never cross again, but yet, for that moment, it was a perfect way to spend my New Year's Eve.

Janice

Janice had not found much success in the relationship department. She was coming to the end of her second marriage. The divorce papers had been filed and many of the decisions regarding division of property and visitation for their child had been ironed out. They were still living in the same house, but she said he was supposedly looking for a new place, although she couldn't be sure. That was how poor the communication had become.

"I have yet to be married to the right guy. I have been married twice and had one child in each marriage. The first marriage lasted ten years and this one lasted about seven," she revealed. "I feel like I always just 'settled' rather than waiting for the right fit."

Janice had been a pretty girl in school. She was chosen for things like homecoming and prom attendant by her classmates. She was a bit on the shy side, but had many friends and was involved in activities. She felt that the defining moment occurred the summer before her senior year in high school.

"I had gone out on a date with this very cute guy from town. When we got back home, I got out of the car. He came around pushed me down into the seat. He raped me right there in my driveway. She confessed. "I felt so helpless. I went inside to the bathroom. I felt so dirty. I didn't dare tell my parents because my father would have murdered the boy. I just threw away my bloodied underwear and hid from the truth. After that, I lost all of my self-confidence."

"That incident just took a lot away from me," she continued. "I just didn't feel worthy after that. What guy would want a girl who had been raped? Why did he do that? It certainly wasn't a very pleasant thing and maybe, deep down I felt it was my fault even though I knew better."

Janice ended up marrying what she would now describe as the wrong type twice. She settled for less than she deserved and ended up facing issues from her spouse from alcohol and drug use and general irresponsibility.

"I remember one night coming home from work; I worked at a grocery store until midnight," Janice recalled. "I came home when my daughter was two and found my husband passed out. He was the only person there to care for the baby. Then one evening, about a year later, I pulled in the driveway and there sat my husband and my three-year-old, both drinking beer. I was furious. This lifestyle was not me."

Janice got to the point in her second marriage where she simply did not care. She had given up on just about every aspect of life but her children. She developed a weight issue and some related health issues and was clearly on a downward spiral. Finally, one day with the help and encouragement of an old friend, she decided that she had had enough. That was six months ago. She filed for divorce. She started eating healthy and exercising. Janice finally took back control of her life. She has lost approximately forty pounds and is getting healthier every day. She is also much better emotionally. Her friends and family are simply amazed at the transformation. All she really did was to decide to stop being the victim and start living again. Once again she is steering her own ship!

Anahid

I found the next house. It was in a middle-class neighborhood north of the city. The name of my rider, Anahid, was unique. I wasn't sure whether to expect a man or woman to be honest. I could see through a blurred storm door window the silhouetted figures hugging and doing the two cheek kisses that you see in certain cultures. Shortly, a middle-aged man opened the door and out popped a dark haired woman in her early thirties I would presume. This, I would learn, was Anahid.

As we began our journey, I broke the ice with the typical politeness about the warmer than usual February weather we were enjoying. Anahid said this had been a perfect day for an outing to visit her friends for dinner. She explained that she was born in Armenia when it was still a part of the old Soviet block of countries. Following the breakup of the Soviet Union, war broke out in her home country, so her family moved to Russia and then emigrated to America when she was just ten-years-old. Even though America has truly been her home, she likes to think of herself as an Armenian woman and tries to preserve Armenian customs. There is not a large Armenian presence in Indiana, so any time she comes across others from her birth country, they are treated like extended family. Such was the case on this evening. The house where I had picked her up was the home of an Armenian family who had befriended her. They had gotten together on this day for a traditional meal.

I asked her to describe to me the "must have" food from her country. She described a ground beef mixture wrapped in grape leaves and said that their foods resembled Greek or Mediterranean cuisine. Understanding, preserving and practicing her culture was an important part of who she is. However, there was much more to this woman than you would suspect at first glance. She went on to tell me that she had worked on Wall Street in the financial industry, but that the Wall Street career lifestyle was not very conducive to a woman who hoped to have a family someday. So, she had changed gears and was now a dentist. I jokingly asked her if she made this move to help people or to inflict pain on others. She offered that many of her friends often commented on what a drastic change in career direction she had taken. She then confessed that the real reason for the change was due to life flexibility. Being a dentist offered her the ability to earn a very good living and still pursue the other things in life that she wanted.

What an inspiration. So many people from much more privileged backgrounds do not achieve half as much as this woman already has in half a life. Born into difficult circumstances, she has found a way to defeat all obstacles that have stood in her way. Most of us, myself included, could learn much from her example.

Another Janice Story

Many of the people I have talked to during the course of making this book have told me the exact same line, "My life is very boring. There is nothing of interest to write about me."

The same was true of my next person. Her name is Janice and she is forty-nine and she swore nothing of interest had ever happened in her life. Well, I am here to tell you that there was a truly profound series of events that happened in her childhood and early adulthood that I am certain shaped the professional, strong, caring and vibrant person she is today.

"My best friend was diagnosed with cancer in the third grade. "Uterine cancer," Janice began. "She would have been what ... eight-years-old at the time?"

It turns out the doctors did surgery, didn't get it all, but then did chemotherapy and treatments and eventually her friend, Corrine, was told she was in remission. The news was a big relief and life was able to go on.

"Corrine and I were always up to something...we got caught playing strip poker once. But the really bad thing happened when we were going to the county fair. Her grandparents lived next door to mine. We were told to go to her grandparent's house and get in the tub so we could go to the fair," Janice smiled. "Well, we were in the tub...we got the bright idea to pour baby oil all over the bathroom floor and go sliding in it. Everyone was next door sitting on my grandparents' porch. They could hear us squealing thru the upstairs window...they came to investigate. Baby oil all over the bathroom floor....we got our asses smacked by more than one set of hands, and we did not go to the fair. That escapade caused them to have to replace the floor ... (laughs) ... that was Corrine and I ... always up to something!!"

"Four years later, I went to her 12th birthday party in May. The 15th I think it was." Janice said. "Later that same month Corrine got the bad news that her cancer had returned. I watched her go downhill from May to December. I was young. I didn't understand what was going on. I watched her hair fall out, the bleeding gums, the wound that would not heal. It scared the crap out of me. I even began to avoid her because I was afraid I would catch the cancer."

Janice explained how she became obsessed with hand washing. She had turned into a self-described hypochondriac. She was obsessed with the fear that she would also catch some germ and get sick. It became a real issue of concern for Janice's parents.

The worst came in mid-December that same year. "I was decorating the Christmas tree when dad took the call. Corrine had died. It was the first time and one of only a few times in my life that I ever saw my dad cry," Janice recalled "I felt very guilty for a long time afterward for how I had avoided Corrine. It was a horrible thing to do, but I was young and didn't understand."

Corrine's mother, I learned, had died of breast cancer at the age of twenty-one. Six months after Corrine passed away, Corrine's father died of lung cancer and a brain tumor. He was thirty-three.

One family—a mother, a father, and a daughter—all died of cancer within a few years of one another at the ages of twelve, twenty-one and thirty-three. Their little family was gone.

The father had been a doctor. It was learned later that he had recognized his own symptoms, ordered the tests and then kept the results a secret. He carried this burden alone. It turns out that this little family had lived, at the time of Corrine's birth, in a town that had been suspect for it's high incidence of disease and illness due to radon gas pollution in that area. Three young, vibrant lives were lost. A whole family just vanished.

Janice had been too young to recall the death of Corrine's mother, but she was heavily touched by the deaths of Corrine and her father. It was a very challenging time as a girl trying to understand life and death on such a scale as this.

As it turned out, tragedy would soon strike again. When Janice was twenty-five, her father, who was forty-seven at the time, began to have episodes of nausea and vomiting after he ate. This issue progressed in frequency over the next couple of months. Finally, it got to the point where he had to go to the doctor. At first they treated him with something for acid reflux. That helped for about twenty-four hours but then the symptoms returned. He was then admitted to the hospital and scheduled for exploratory surgery.

"I was living and working in another state at the time," Janice explained. "I remember mom called and said that dad had pancreatic cancer and was going to die. They gave him six to twelve months to live."

"I remember the first words out of my mouth were, Oh My God! He is never going to be a grandpa!" she continued, "I was the oldest child and Daddy's girl. I had just started a new job and did not get to come home much, but I remember how quickly he went downhill. I now saw this big, strong man shuffling around like someone twice his age. He only lasted about one and a half months and then he was gone."

Needless to say, Janice was devastated and admitted that she still cries sometimes twenty-four years later. Cancer is a six letter word of evil that has played a major role in shaping Janice's life. She has been made stronger by these tragedies she has faced. I am sure her daddy would be proud. Losing a friend at age twelve and her father at age twenty-five is more than many of us would ever hope to face. I hope that today you take the time to make that phone call or give that hug because you have no promise that tomorrow will give you that same opportunity.

✳✳✳

Why do you care what I think? Well, honestly, you shouldn't. You are very capable of your own thoughts and ideas. When I give my perspective or opinions, it should not diminish yours. My job is just to get you thinking. When I reminisce about my childhood or a situation I have encountered, I want it to spark a memory of your own and hopefully put a smile on your face. I am lucky to have that job. I am lucky to be the bearer of good news.

In life, we have many resources to learn about the bad stuff in the world. I think we need to connect, more frequently, to the laughter and the humanity and decency that exist in every corner of our planet. It is by giving the best of what we are that we can accomplish more than we could ever imagine.

Woman Talk

Women talk funny. No, I don't mean to say they sound funny, well some of them do. For instance, my friend, Meg, had a very strong southern drawl. She made two or three syllables out of one all the time. She would say things like he-yer for here and they-yer for there. It seems like she had to work twice as hard as the rest of us to say the same thing. Well, not as hard as deaf people do I suppose. Speaking American Sign Language is physical speech. If you talk too much your arms get tired … hmmm … maybe all women should use sign language! I spent several years around deaf people on a daily basis and I can sign okay, enough to get along. Even in their community, there are great differences in signing styles. Some are very conservative and to the point, others sign with great flair and flamboyant motions, very animated signing you might say. I guess it is really the same as how people talk differently.

Where was I? Oh yes, women talk funny. I started to become aware of this from texting, but I noticed that even in person, this is how women speak. Let me give you an example. First, I will portray a man's version via text.

Man: OMG! I was late for a doctor's appointment to get my test results and then there was this huge dump truck that got tangled in some overhead electrical wires and caused a traffic jam. I had to take a detour out past the place where Elizabeth works just to get to the doctor. Fortunately, they were running behind and the test results came out normal.

Okay, now same exact story in woman's version text.

Woman: OMG! . . . . (okay now I have waited for ten minutes for her to continue)

Woman: Are U there?

Me: Yes

Woman: This was not what I needed

. . . .(five more minutes pass)

Me: Needed for what?

Woman: Oh, it's okay now. I was stressed there for a minute.

Me: About what?

Woman: Oh, by the way, I saw Elizabeth today.

Me: Oh really? How is she? And why were you stressed?

Woman: Well, I didn't talk to her, I was just driving by that place where she works and I saw her standing in the parking lot talking to some other people.

Me: Oh okay.

. . . .(waiting for woman to continue) . . . . (one hour has passed)

Me: Are you going to tell me why you were so stressed earlier?

Woman: It was all because of the stupid truck. I didn't need the hassle today.

Me: I didn't realize you owned a truck

Woman: NO! Dummy! There was this big dump truck. He knocked down a bunch of electrical wires and made me late.

Me: Late for what?

. . . . (waiting again)

. . . .
. . . . (ten minutes)

Me: What were you late for?

Woman: My doctor's appointment. He was giving me my test results today.

Me: Oh, okay

. . . .(waiting for her to continue)

. . . .
(five minutes) . . . .

Woman: Well, aren't you going to ask me about the results? Or don't you even care?

Me: I have been waiting

Woman: Waiting for what?

Me: Never mind

Woman: So you don't want to know if I am going to live or die?

Me: Yes. Please tell me!

Woman: He said I am fine! Not that you seem to care!

Ugh!

A Rekindling

He was forty-four. It was nearly midnight. He entered my car with a smile and a friendly greeting. He was headed home from this restaurant/pub located in a northern middle-class suburb. He asked me to pull the car around to the other side of the building for a minute so that he could tell a friend that his ride had arrived. There, in the parking lot, in a dark SUV, sat a smiling forty-four-year-old woman. They both rolled down their windows.

"See you later! I love you!" the man called out.

"I love you too! We will talk more tomorrow!" she replied.

It did appear to me, on the surface, odd that she was not driving him home instead of me, but who was I to ask questions? I needed to be much more sneaky about it and get him to feel as if he were volunteering the information I desired! He, like most of my passengers, asked how I liked driving rideshares. I told him how I loved meeting all of the people and the interesting stories that each of them shared with me (hint, hint). I told him about the woman who was leaving her boyfriend and about the girl who was making amends with her estranged mother who now had cancer. I was pulling at his heart strings. It worked.

"Well, I think I should open up and share my story with you too," he began. "That woman back there? I fell in love with her twenty-five years ago. We worked at the same store together when we were teenagers. We dated for about a year and then she just ran away. I assumed that she just didn't feel the same way that I did. Life went on. We married other people. But, I never forgot her. Two weeks ago, I ran into her again. I am single. She is going through a divorce. We talked. It turns out that she had always felt the same way about me too, but she ran away all of those years ago because she got scared of all of those feelings at age nineteen. If I had only known! We have decided to try what we should have tried twenty-five years ago. We are dating again. I always felt that she was where I belonged and now I get a second chance."

He talked about regretting the missed years with her, but he also knew that maybe, for some unknown reason, this was how it was supposed to work out. He seemed like a nice guy and I wished him well. Once again, I truly believe that everybody has a story.

I'm Hot

I pulled up in front of a newly opened "experience" restaurant that had opened near the mall. Two women and two men appearing to be in their mid-twenties piled in, the guys and one girl in the back, and a very attractive blue eyed, blonde landed in the passenger seat.

"Hi, how are you?" she smiled. "Dang, you sure are cute! You've got that sort of quirky, sexy thing going on!"

Her friends in the back seat were laughing at her obviously inebriated ramblings. She went on to tell me that the other three were triplets and that she was home on holiday and had gone out to dinner with them. She asked me what I did besides drive. I told her I was a writer and that I write true stories of people's lives. She immediately volunteered to be one of my subjects. She proceeded to tell me how her boyfriend had unceremoniously dumped her on her birthday and how he didn't even seem to feel bad about it. She then went back and forth about whether this turn of events had been hurtful to her or not.

It wasn't long before she was sound asleep and snoring, leaning on my shoulder as we finished the drive home. The whole trip left me wondering, "Am I really that sexy or was she just really drunk?" Aw, who am I kidding? I am really that sexy!

✳✳✳

Four grown men took my rideshare car on a thirty-minute ride to downtown. The discussion topics were budget goals for the month at work, salary bonus, the dangers of foreign strip clubs, football, baseball, words in other languages that have no direct translation into English, the unmanliness of going to Twin Peaks (sorta like Hooters) and ordering a salad and water, losing a testicle, and Jimmy Fallon.

Three grown women took a twenty-five-minute rideshare in my car to downtown. The discussion topics were other women they work with, chocolate, my hair, why Jason won't pop the question already, where to buy shoes, where the Indianapolis Colts players live, what to pack for a trip to Cancun next week, things you should never do for love, and nails.

Oh Those Changes

I have been walking around this world for just over fifty years. If you are eighteen, you will say that I am ancient. If you are seventy-five, you will say I am just a baby. Perspective is everything. I have been examining my life and thinking about the things that were not around when I was a kid that are commonplace now. Some are easy to see, others are a bit surprising to me. I also have started thinking about the things that were commonplace and are now just a part of history that children today will never truly experience as I once did. So, here are my two lists. I am certain that you will be able to add your own things to these lists, but at least this is a start.

Things that have appeared in my lifetime (some of these were around prior to me, but they appeared in my world at a later date):

*McDonalds

(Here is a good example. Founded in 1955, but the first one I ever saw was in 1969.)

*Microwave Ovens

(Mom still uses the one she bought in 1981. No wonder she has a glow about her.)

*Personal/Home/Laptop Computers
(Curt had one that took a good thirty minutes to load a program in the … early 1980's.)
*Bottled Water
(Who would have ever dreamed of paying for the stuff?)
*Energy Drinks
*Color Television
(Or even a TV over 21".)
*CD/Digital Music
(Is the sound really better?)
*SUV
(We had pickups and full sized vans and station wagons!)
*Cellular Phones
(This is a big one. We are so hooked.)
*The Internet
(A game changer.)
*Organic Food
(How did we ever survive without it?)
*Air Conditioned Homes
(I am sure it was invented, but nobody I knew had it.)
*Dishwasher
(We all had dishpan hands.)
*Laundry/Dishwasher Pods and Liquid Detergents
(They were all powders.)
*Airport Security
(Well, they were there but kind of like the security guards at the mall.)
*Professional Sports Cheerleaders
(Yes! What a great thing! I looked it up. The Cowboys cheerleaders were first introduced in 1972.)

*Tofurkey

(Wrap it in a slice of bacon and it's not half bad.)

*All Wheel Drive/ Antilock Brakes/ Airbags

(Airbags to us were certain little old ladies at church. Our cars even had steel dashboards.)

*WalMart

(The first WalMart actually opened in 1962 in Arkansas, but I was an adult before I ever encountered one. I remember their first commercials were touting the fact that they sold predominately American-made products. Gee, I don't hear that anymore!)

*Pooper Scooper

(Maybe some people scooped poop, but where I grew up, if somebody's dog went in your yard, it was just tough shit.)

*Video Games

(Pong was the first. Blips on a screen. We spent hours! Space Invaders followed. Talk about High Tech!)

*Cordless Tools

(No plug, no drill.)

*Wireless remotes

(We actually had to walk across the floor to switch between our three channels! Pure Torture!)

*Debit Cards

(Money is nearly obsolete now.)

Things That Have Faded into History

*8 Track Tapes and Albums

(Albums still do have a nostalgic following and are still maybe the purest sound ... if it weren't for those darned scratches.)

*Space Food Sticks

(What? You don't remember those? I gave one to Curt in the fourth grade. We have been best friends ever since.)

*Wired Remotes

(An upgrade from walking across the floor.)

*Glass Bottle Deposits

(Maybe somewhere still, but I remember hauling bottles to the store for money!)

*Outhouses

(Yes, I have used them. I think my children would explode first.)

*Leisure Suits

(Hey, maybe they will make a comeback!)

*Typewriters

(Especially the manual ones. And don't make a mistake at the bottom of the page.)

*Subaru Brat

(If you are too young to recall, this was the first four passenger truck, like an extended cab, except the rear seats were rear facing, resembled lawn chairs and were outdoors, bolted in the bed of the truck. Oh, to be a kid whose parents owned one of these when it was raining or worse, snowing! We were all about safety back then!)

*Mimeograph

(They used one in elementary school. The first thing every kid did was smell the paper!)

*Adding Machine

(Especially the ones where you chose the hundreds, then the tens, then the ones, etc. ...)

*Foil TV Dinners

(Heck they were ready in only 30-40 minutes.)

*Soda Can Tabs

(They were littered everywhere just waiting to slice open a bare foot.)

*Wooden Tennis Rackets
(Had to store them in a brace to prevent warping.)
*G.C Murphy's
(Toys, records and warm cashews. They had other stuff too, but that was what was important to me.)
*K-Tel Commercials
(All those compilation albums we just had to have.)
*The Sears Wishbook
(I would wear that thing out every year.)

These are just a few things off the top of my head. Feel free to add your own.

Jaz

I choose the people I interview for a variety of reasons. The bottom line is always because they stand out from the crowd for one reason or another. I chose this woman for two reasons. The first reason was that she had a beautiful, outgoing and positive personality. The second reason was because if I were ever in a fight with her, I was reasonably certain that she could kick my ass. Was she six-foot-seven and three hundred pounds? Hardly! But I do recall the first time that I ever saw her. She had her feet up on a bench and her hands down on the floor doing boy pushups! The first words I ever said to her were, "You scare me!" She just laughed and a friendship was born.

Jaz is just naturally a very attractive woman. She doesn't do much of anything in the way of makeup or special hairstyles. She said that she doesn't even really know how. It's just not a priority for her. She is impressed with women who can do that, but she never learned how to 'paint her face' like that. Jaz also is one of these people who just oozes positive energy. She is smiling and energetic and approachable. People just randomly get involved in extended conversations with her about anything. Next, Jaz is very fit. She has an athletic, muscular physical appearance that is impressive. She is not what you would call a bodybuilder with overbuilt muscles. She just looks amazingly fit and toned. So, from the outside, this thirty-year-old woman has so much going for her. I needed to know what makes her tick.

"I am a single mom of a four-year-old little boy who is my biggest motivator in the whole world. We work well together. It's just he and I so we don't live by strict rules, we just do what needs to be done," Jaz smiled. "I am an accountant. I bet you would have never guessed that! Me … closed up in a cubicle all day!"

I asked Jaz to tell me about what life was like for her growing up.

"My Mom and Dad got divorced when I was three and mom remarried when I was four. My real dad had me every other weekend. He never missed those visitations. He always came. I was never the kid crying at the door because daddy didn't show up again. Those weekends were great. But he also never went out of his way either. I was very involved in everything from T-ball through softball and was good at it and I also competed in dance nationally. I can only recall Dad coming to one ball game in all of those years and that was because it was right up the street from his house. Many of my games were within a few miles, but he just never seemed to make the effort," Jaz recalled.

"Now, my step-dad was awesome." she continued. "He and my mom are still together twenty-what? Twenty-six years later. I became very close to him. You see my mom was an alcoholic. She wasn't always there for me. She had major problems. It was so bad that I had to memorize my grandparents' phone number and at times, when things got really bad, I would run to the neighbors' house and make a call for Mamaw to come and get me. But, my Step-Dad stood by me. He took care of me when my mom could not. I remember how he made my sweet sixteen birthday special even though my mom was not around. She had disappeared and left us for three months. My Step-Dad could have just left too. He had no obligation to me. But, he stayed right there and took care of me."

Jaz perked up, "Mom is sober now! She went from going out drinking, to staying home drinking and finally, when the doctor told her that it was affecting her liver function, she quit cold turkey. The same thing happened with her and smoking. As soon as the doctor mentioned signs of Emphysema, she stopped. I hate to say this (laughing), but I am glad she had those things happen if it gave me my Mom back! See, Mom loves Christmas and she was always sober on Christmas morning. I now like to say that it's now ALWAYS Christmas morning when I am with Mom!"

I then moved into asking Jaz about how she had ended up so differently. She talked about how her grandparents had played a big role in establishing her goals and values and that they had developed a plan of how she could get out and go to college and make a conscious choice not to give in to that lifestyle.

"I made the decision to fall into good things instead of alcoholism" she said.

Life was not a cake walk for Jaz. She had to work and go to school and stay busy and focused. The worst year was when she was twenty-four.

"I tried out to be an NFL cheerleader that year. I was on my own. I didn't have any friends doing it, but I made many friends at cheerleader camp. I made it all the way to the last round before the Showcase, which is the last cut before the finals. They group you off by height. If you notice at a game, you have girls of similar height performing together around the stadium. It looks odd if you have tall girl, short girl, tall girl. And of course they want diversity.

When they put us all into our final height groups, I looked around and saw two veteran cheerleaders in the group who looked like me. I knew I was done! I should have tried out again the next year, but a lot happened in that time," Jaz continued.

"I didn't know it at the time of the tryouts, but I was very early in a pregnancy. I was not married, but the father and I had been together for a couple of years. I got excited. I saw the ultrasound, heard the heartbeat. At eleven weeks, I finally made the trip down to my grandparents' house to tell them the news. I was apprehensive, because I was not married, as to how they would respond. As it turned out, they were very excited too! The very next day, at work, I started bleeding. They took me in for an ultrasound and although the tech was not permitted to tell me, I knew the baby was dead. The doctor gave me the choice of having a D&C or to take a pill to cause contractions and expel the remnants of the pregnancy at home. The doctor encouraged me to do the at home method and it was horrible. I sat in the bathtub amidst a lot of bloody clots. There was one particular larger clot that you could just tell was the broken down remains of my baby." Jaz paused slightly. "When I went back to the doctor she said to me, 'The product has passed.' She used this terminology about three different times. Finally, I told her that this 'Product' that she kept referring to, was my child. The father was right there with me through all of this and he even cleaned up the tub for me! We remained together and two years later we did have a son. We stayed together another year after that before separating for good. He is sporadically in our son's life, but nothing I can count on."

Jaz had more to offer, "Shortly after the miscarriage, I was called into the doctor's office and told I had stage III precancerous tumors on my cervix. I had to have those lasered. I was totally devastated by the miscarriage having heard the heartbeat and everything, and then the cancer scare. Next, a few weeks later, came tachycardia. My heartbeat became so fast that the staff at the hospital said I was in danger of a stroke. They gave me this injection and my whole body just went limp. It was a very strange sensation!"

Jaz had some doctor visits and they tried to prescribe her anti anxiety/depression medications, but she simply had an aversion to taking them and as life improved, her symptoms lessened. She talked about how she now has a 'rescue' pill in case she feels an attack coming on, but other than that she is fine.

She has gone on to get a Masters degree, thanks in part to her grandparents who would come to her house and cook meals and stay until late in the evening so that Jaz could get her coursework completed. She has bought a house and has become more active in fitness competitions.

"Where did the bodybuilding begin?" I asked

"When I was in college, I met a man who owned a gym and he and a woman who worked there as a trainer encouraged me. I had always been athletic, but that was when I began to weight train. They were the ones that taught me the names of different exercises and how nutrition fits into the equation. I learned so much from them."

Jaz went on to explain that there are various types of bodybuilding and competitions. She even talked about how her grandmother was concerned that she was going to get 'too big'. Jaz has started competing and just recently qualified for a national competition by finishing third in her state. The term for what she does is figure competitions. She even hopes to maybe get her Pro Card one day. She would also like to pursue fitness modeling. She said that she had done catalog and magazine modeling in the past, but nothing fitness related.

"I once had a lady come up to me at the gym asking for tips." Jaz chuckled. "She said that she wanted to get toned but that she didn't want to look like me! My goal is muscular, not manly. Some people have referred to me as a 'Figure Chick'"

I wanted to know what life was like for a very fit and attractive young woman.

"Well, I do get lots of private messages and such when I post competition photos. But they usually start out 'Hey Sexy' or 'Looking good, gorgeous!' I can usually spot those ones fairly quick. Mostly I have dated friends of friends so I kind of knew their backgrounds. There was this one guy who didn't come to me that way and it turned out that he was married. I told him that was so unfair that he didn't even tell me and give me the chance to make my own decisions about that! What really sucked is that he and I had been great friends and we communicated all of the time! So, I stopped dating him, but kept him as a friend I talked to. But, then a few months later, I found out that he had even lied to me about his name!" Jaz seemed to take it all in stride.

"What about the future?" I asked

"Well, aside from the figure competitions, I want to find a different job. I want to work to live, not live to work. Did I get that right or was that backwards?" Laughing, she explained, "I also want to provide a good life for my son and maybe move somewhere warmer (smiles). I am not afraid of much. I am not afraid of dying or getting older. One thing that will bother me is when my grandparents pass away. I have never been through the death of anyone close to me. That is going to be hard. My Mamaw has asked me what things I want and I told her nothing! I don't want to talk about it! All I want is her here with me. I also know that I need to spend more time with them now before it's too late."

I jumped in and nudged her a bit, "You mentioned that you are not afraid to die. Tell me about your beliefs."

""Um, I think I am more spiritual than religious. I wasn't raised in a religious environment. I really don't know much about things in the Bible." she offered. "I began going to a church about six months ago and I enjoy how the positive message leaves me feeling when I leave. I feel ready to face the day. I do believe there is a higher power, but I don't like when you tell somebody about your troubles and they say, 'It's okay, God will take care of it'. I feel like saying, "So, if I just go over there and sit on the couch, then God will handle it from there?' I believe you need to play an active role in resolving issues in your life and prayer can be a great part of that."

Jaz is currently rehabbing from a surgical procedure on her knee from an injury she incurred while playing flag football. She lamented how she now notices details more and is frustrated by a decrease in definition in her leg muscles due to the time off. I have no doubt that she will be back to 100% in not time at all.

My overall impression of Jaz was awesome. She is such a positive role model of how you do not need to be a product of your upbringing. She did not allow herself to fall into the pit of alcoholism as her mother had done. Sure, she had people who helped her along the way. Sure she had positive influences. But, Jaz is a self-made vibrant woman, beautiful inside and out. She is so unique. Her rare mix of personality, beauty, and strength, along with that can-do attitude, makes her one of the most unforgettable people I have ever gotten to know.

You go Jaz!

Bread Wars

On my way home today I stopped by the Farmers Market that they have every Thursday afternoon in the church parking lot up the street from my house. The market runs April through September and has a variety of vendors offering their fruits and vegetables and baked goods etc. … Being that we are now into the back half of September, there is only today and next week left for this year. On top of that, the bread man told me last week that he would not be here the final week of the market, so today would be my last time to get that fabulous homemade Kodiak bread he brings. He bakes his breads fresh the day of the market and there is only a limited supply of each kind.

There was an unfortunate episode a few weeks ago when I got delayed and arrived at his stand just as this mean old lady with a walker was buying his last loaf of MY bread! I even tried to explain to her that I ALWAYS bought this bread and that this guy was my ONLY supplier.

She just looked at me and smiled and said, "Well, I guess not today!"

Old Witch! I had to wait an extra week and I was NOT happy about it! I made certain to be early every Thursday from then on. I was not going to be put in that situation again! But, as luck would have it, today I needed to run by an ATM for some cash before I got to the market. As I was driving past the market, I saw that old witch getting out of her car! Crap! I didn't have my money yet and she looked hungry for bread! Now, no need to bore you with details, but all you need to know is that I made it to the ATM and back to the market. I rushed up to the bread man and halleluiah, I got his last loaf! Just as I was receiving my cherished prize the old witch showed up asking for the same. She was out of luck and furious.

She said, "I would have been here before you except some idiot ran over my walker with their car as I was getting my purse out of the seat! I think you should let me have that loaf of bread since I was here first!"

I just looked at her and smiled, "Well, I guess not today!"

✳✳✳

A true story as told by one of my Facebook friends about a conversation she recently had with her child.

Child: Mom, how do cows get bread?

Mother: Bread? Honey, I don't think cows use bread.

Child: Well, grandpa said that the cows were going to get bread soon.

Mother: Hmm … I think you need to have grandpa to explain that one to you!

The Story Behind the Face

I had met this beautiful forty-five-year-old woman a few years ago through her mother. I had always been curious about her life and finally had the opportunity to ask her for an interview. I gave her a few days to think about it and she said yes. I was thrilled. The reason I was happy about this one was because I already knew she had a story. I didn't know the details, but I knew that she had been through a unique experience. What clued me in? Let me back up just a pinch. This woman, as I mentioned, was very attractive, professional, with a kind personality. She was a vibrant, single African American woman chasing her dreams. She appeared to have a gentle strength. In one word, I always found her impressive. But there was an interesting, though not particularly noticeable, long thin scar across the side of her neck. That scar had to carry a story with it. So, one day I asked her about it. That was when I knew I had to tell her story.

The event related to her scar had occurred in her early thirties. She was able to recount the events that day with great clarity.

"It was around four or five in the afternoon on May 15th," she began. "I needed to make a stop on my way home at the grocery store. At that time of day, it was very busy. I noticed a car at the very end of the parking lot when I came in, but really didn't pay it much attention. With the lot very full, I had to park a long way from the store. I parked and got out and then turned to reach back into my car for my purse. The car that had been at the end of the lot pulled up closer and an older black man came up from behind. I never heard what it was he said, but I suddenly felt something against my throat and as I fell back into the driver's seat, I was fighting him off. He was after my purse."

In the end, the man did get the purse. He jumped back into the car driven by an older Hispanic man and they sped away. Her adrenaline was running so high that she had not experienced any pain or even realized that she had been injured. It turns out she had been cut by a knife and sustained cuts along the left side of her throat. The side of her face leading toward her mouth was punctured clear through from just below her cheekbone to the inside of her mouth and her hand and fingers were also lacerated. She later learned that she had been the third victim of these robbers that day. Another woman had been cut across the lips. The third victim, a man, had fought them off thwarting their efforts.

"There was a woman who witnessed what had happened to me," she continued. "This woman didn't have a cell phone or anything, but she followed the getaway car for a ways and saw them throw my purse out the window. She even got a license plate number."

The reason the thieves had dumped the purse was because there was nothing of value inside. As luck would have it, the coin purse, which contained cash and credit cards, had fallen out in her car during the struggle. The thieves had gotten away with nothing and now someone could identify them.

She then recounted the emergency room visit, "This was where my torture began. The adrenaline had died down. The pain had surfaced. The medical staff could not put me to sleep because I could not recall the last time I had eaten. As I said, I did not feel getting cut, but the getting numbed was horrible! They had to stick me again and again and again along my mouth, the side of my face and my neck. I was also given Morphine in an IV for the pain."

The doctors told her that she was lucky to be alive. The knife wound on her neck had narrowly missed her jugular vein. She was stitched up and released from the hospital later that evening. When she finally got home, she threw up. Stitches all over her face and neck and throwing up. That's enough to make you cringe. She also endured painful neck and face injections over the healing period to lessen the scars.

What happened to the crooks? "The good Samaritan was able to identify the attacker through a lineup. The case went to court. The day of court, the Samaritan was in the hospital with pregnancy complications. Without the state's key eyewitness, the case was thrown out," she lamented. "I never heard another word about it and never saw justice served."

Tickets

I watched an NFL football game on television yesterday. It was the Baltimore Ravens visiting the Cincinnati Bengals. It was a good, competitive game. Both teams were battling for first place in their division. The weather was nice and sunny, a pretty Fall day. The stadium was filled with a sellout crowd. The Bengals led 17-6 midway through the third quarter, but Baltimore didn't give up. With six minutes left in the fourth, Baltimore had taken a one point lead 21-20. The Bengals got the ball back, but fumbled setting up a Baltimore field goal. The score was now 24-20 Baltimore with 3minutes fifty-nine seconds remaining on the game clock. That is still a lot of time in football time! The television cameras showed the throngs of Cincinnati fans heading for the parking lot. This made me scratch my head. The home team was trailing by less than a touchdown with nearly four minutes left to play. These people had paid big money and driven to the game, yet they were not interested in waiting to see the finish? What? Did they want to avoid traffic? Well, then why not just stay at home and watch on the television? Do they not pay to go to a game to watch it? Now I could understand if it were a blowout, but this was a game still undecided!

I got curious so I pulled up the average 2014 ticket prices for the NFL games. Cincinnati was $195.46. That was the average that people paid per person to leave early and listen to the ending on a car radio. Considering most people take a friend and eat something and buy gas to get there, these folks averaged spending $500 to miss the ending. It parallels going to a movie and leaving fifteen minutes before they tell you who killed the butler or driving all but the last three miles to work and then just getting out and walking the rest of the way even if it gets you in trouble for being late. Anyhow, back to these ticket prices. Cincinnati is a bargain. Actually Cleveland had the lowest average price at $146.53, a good twenty dollars cheaper than the next lowest, Oakland Raiders. The most expensive average? That would be the Super Bowl Champion Seattle Seahawks at an average ticket price of $452.34. That's an easy way to drop a thousand dollars with food and gas and a friend.

So, anyway, these people in Cincinnati who left early, did they miss anything? Their team came back to win 27-24 in a nail biter of a finish that included one of the best one-handed catches I have ever seen to keep a drive alive. They missed what was essentially the best part of the game.

I shouldn't be surprised, I guess. People are always in a rush to get to the next big thing that they often miss out on some great moments. Stop along the way and enjoy life. Don't always be rushing to beat the crowd.

∗∗∗

If you have ever changed a cat's litter box, then you know that there can be a strong ammonia smell. Well, this morning I was mopping the bathroom floor with ammonia when our cat, Smokey, appeared around the corner. He took one whiff and looked at me as if to say, "My God human! Are you sick or something? There is a perfectly good litter box downstairs for that!!!"

He then turned and trotted down the hallway, I could almost hear him saying, "FuzzButt! FuzzButt! Our human just peed all over the scary water room! OMG! The smell will make your eyes water!"

☝

Catnip Confessions

FuzzButt has finally admitted that he has a catnip "problem". He simply doesn't seem to be able to use it responsibly. He lacks self-control. And once he gets a snort of the stuff, he acts as if he can conquer the world. He picks fights with everybody including Goldie, who is twice his size. She could simply sit on him and he would be a goner. He even tries to wrestle with Smoky, which would be like me versus a grizzly bear. He then stands up on the sofa and begins twerking and teasing the others. He is a real piece of work! Right now I can see him on the very top of the cat tree, his head and paw are hanging over the edge. He is staring down at Smoky and calling him names. Oh no! I think he just called him a schnauzer! Smoky is heading up the tree! Poor FuzzButt! He is in for a butt whippin now!

%&%(*)^%^&$&(*)(**()&%$&^ ……..

Greetings readers! FuzzButt here! I just dove off the top shelf of my treehouse and surprise attacked my servant. I could see he was writing hateful things about me again! I DO NOT, I repeat, I DO NOT have a catnip problem! I can hold my catnip as good as the next chap and still find my way home. Besides, what is wrong with a snort or two after a hard day? And what better way to unwind with friends than with some fresh, PetSmart vintage. I really do not see the problem here. I am not hurting anyone… well, except for that one time when I was under the influence and sauntering across the counter and that burning candle jumped out and bit my tail. They tried to blame that on me and the catnip, but it was obviously the candle's fault! They also got on my case about the time I knocked over the plant and nearly killed Spooky. Now, would that have really been such a great loss? She is always cranky and bossy anyhow! The humans say I need a twelve step program. I really don't know what they mean by that, if it is an exercise program then they can just forget it. I need my nap time. They need to realize who is the TRUE boss around here and the soo ……..

()*^)*(&&%(&^$%$##$)*()()_()(&^%%$

Sorry about that folks. We had another "issue" here with FuzzButt. But it is all under control for the moment. He has been temporarily incarcerated in the cat carrier. The other cats are walking around the thing and taunting him now. Smoky just told him that he'd better be glad he is in there because once he gets ahold of FuzzButt there will be hairballs to pay! I had better go for now. This is getting serious!

A Child

A child is a child. I don't care if a child was born rich or poor, to Christian or Muslim parents, in rural America or some large metropolis in western Asia. They are just a kid. They didn't choose where, when, or into what circumstances they would be born. That was just the environment with which they were presented. So, should it really matter, when children need help, where they are from, what color they are, if their families have money or what we would see as good morals? Should they be judged based upon the environment into which they were born? Is that fair? What sort of circumstances were you given to navigate due to your birth? Are you one of the luckier ones? Did you deserve that privilege more than others? If you reaped the rewards of your ancestors, should you also pay for their sins?

Nerves

One of the things I inherited from my father was a 'nerve problem.' As a kid, I never fully understood what dad meant when he said his 'nerves were shot'. I also didn't understand why he would sometimes become emotional and apprehensive when it was time to go somewhere to a social function or to do a show (he was also a professional musician). I didn't love him any less. I just accepted that dad didn't like it when he had to be at a certain place at a certain time. Ninety-nine percent of the time mom would coax him into going anyway and once he got there, he would get through it. I could tell that sometimes it wasn't fun for him and other times he was okay. This issue was not something he really talked about other than the occasional comment that the war, WWII, had caused it. I figured that being shot at on a regular basis for a few years was enough to make anybody nervous.

As a child growing up, I never really experienced any more than the typical moments of anxiety due to a monster under my bed or a boogie man outside my window. But, as I got older, I began to see other symptoms that would come and go. There were times I would feel tension in the muscles of my neck that would lead to headaches or the feeling that my chest was tightening. I blamed caffeine. I stopped drinking the stuff. It helped. Problem solved, for a while. These moments would later reappear from time to time, but I managed to get through them.

In late 2001, at the age of thirty-nine, life was rolling along. I had owned a successful business for several years, my kids were growing and happy and I really was doing fine. But, I began to have this foreboding feeling deep inside me. It was just always there, slowly increasing, growing. I could not figure it out. I thought maybe it was stress. I thought maybe it was something in my diet. I tried changing various things. Nothing worked. As this feeling grew, I began to feel uncomfortable in my own body. This feeling just would not subside. I now understood a phrase my father had often used saying he just wanted to 'jump out of his own skin'. I now felt that way too. I went to the doctor, she ran a couple of tests to rule out anything major and then she gave me a mild 'nerve pill' to take as needed. That pill did nothing but make me sick to my stomach. I was frustrated.

I began to notice that this ever constant feeling was even worse when I was in a public setting. I was finding myself limiting my time inside a grocery store or in a crowd. After just a few minutes in one of these situations, when I returned to the car, it felt like every muscle in my body was on the verge of a spasm. I found myself retreating into my house more and more. Next I was confining myself to only certain rooms of the house. My world was getting smaller and smaller. The sad part was that I loved people and loved being out there and involved, but my stupid body kept telling me no!

Probably one of the worst moments in my entire life came in April of 2002. I had a couple of errands to run. I was anxious about it from the start. I needed a few things from the grocery and then

I needed to run by the post office. I had by then figured out that if I could be in and out of the grocery store in fifteen minutes, then I could at least handle the building stress. So, that was my game plan. I entered the store, hurriedly got my things and made my way to the checkouts. Of course, there were only a couple of lanes open and naturally, busy. Of course, I picked the lane that needed a price check and such. My tension kept building. By the time I made it back outside to the car, the internal stress was at a full boil. I remember thinking, 'it's okay now! I made it!' But, I just couldn't shake the tension. I started the car and pulled out of the parking lot and into the street. Suddenly every nerve ending in my body felt like it was firing an electrical shock simultaneously. I can only describe it as similar to the feeling when you get a chill except that it felt like electricity. Then, as I pulled up to the next stop light, it happened. Instantly, my heart literally felt as if it was in my throat and it was pounding at two hundred beats per minute so hard that I could feel it all over my body. The sound of the pounding was loud enough to drown out all other noises. My only thought was 'this is it, I am a dead man!' I felt I only had one chance. I was about a mile from a hospital emergency room. I turned on my emergency flashers and ran every red light in my path. I got to hospital, pulled right up front, jumped out of my car, ran inside and told the nurse, "I think I am having a heart attack!" She took one look at me, handed me a clipboard and told me to sit down and fill out the forms and they would be with me in a few minutes. WHAT? DID SHE NOT HEAR ME?

She heard me just fine. She had seen this same scenario before. She knew what a full blown panic attack looked like. My blood pressure that day was 195/110. They gave me some pill that made everything right with the world. My blood pressure was then 127/72. I was going to survive. This event opened the door for more panic attacks. They were miserable and scary. The feelings and sensations were so real and intense. The doctor started me on other daily drugs and also gave me an emergency pill for when the worst symptoms hit. That pill was my lifeline. I knew that fifteen minutes after a big attack, I could feel total bliss. The actual attacks would change. I went through uncontrollable full body shaking and the electrical feeling and numbness, chest tightness, hyperventilation, the works. It was a miserable experience.

One of the worst things about this affliction is that people who have never had it, simply do not understand it. I had several people say, "Oh, I have had a panic attack. They are not that big a deal." Well, I have had those also, but those are NOTHING like the ones I experienced. I always knew when I was talking to someone who had indeed experienced the big ones. You could see it in their knowing eyes as they shared their own story. Also, some people could simply not understand. You weren't bleeding. You didn't have a fever. You had no outward signs of a problem, yet you were incapacitated. So frustrating!

Some people get these conditions and spend the rest of their lives suffering from them. I was one of the lucky ones. I read, I studied and I fought hard. I even had the help of a therapist, Dr. Bowie, to understand that part of the problem for me was that I was a control freak when it came to my surroundings. In public, my surroundings were too big to be controlled. Also, I learned that leading up to an attack, my focus was internal. If I focused on something outside of my own body, I could combat the on-coming attack. I found a great tool for this was video games. It was hard to focus on Mario playing tennis and my pounding heart at the same time. Over time I was able to learn to recognize the symptoms early and simply dismiss them before they grew into anything major. I now live a full and complete life and enjoy getting out into the world and exploring. I now also understand my father better. I know what he lived through and suffered through. Like me, he found ways to cope and to have a fruitful, long life. But, of all the things I inherited from him, this is the one thing I would gladly have lived without!

So, why was this on my mind this morning? Well, because as I sat down to write this story, I was getting past that old familiar feeling of an attack trying to come on. I simply recognized it for what it was and dismissed it, therefore taking away all of its power over me. It may sound silly, but it is the truth and it works! So today, yet again, I won my battle with anxiety and panic attacks!

☝

Enjoy the Journey

Each year we see Christmas show up earlier and earlier in our lives. I would think that there must be a point that this cannot cross. I wonder what is that drop dead date? Before what date can we not tolerate a Christmas advertisement or a Christmas movie or a Christmas song? When I was young, it was at some point after Thanksgiving. Now, it has bowled over Veterans Day and even Halloween. You now see Christmas decorations in many stores in September and even a few in August! All of this buildup for one day. Now, I realize that there is a season of parties and baking, a feel good time. I just wonder if we are selling ourselves short. Why not put some of this energy into the celebration of other holidays? Host a family Halloween party! Invite all of the Vets in your family over and surprise them with gifts and a family meal! Thanksgiving too! It's not just supposed to be about turkey. This is supposed to be a time to give thanks for a good year and hang out with family!

Now, I get the religious perspective of Christmas and I do not wish to belittle its meaning in any way. Where I take issue is the commercialization. This is the part that has overwhelmed our lives. This is the reason we are Christmasing from August forward. Christmas has even stolen Thanksgiving as a holiday from many people. Those who work retail no longer have a Thanksgiving holiday. Is that fair? I don't believe it is. We each need to live our lives by our own standards, but I would not go shopping on Thanksgiving. I would feel I was contributing to the problem. I can find some other time to shop in that month prior to the holiday. I am betting that the upper level managers and board members of these companies open on Thanksgiving are not having their holiday interrupted, yet they are the ones who will reap the biggest rewards. That bothers me on a human level.

I am personally making a deliberate effort to celebrate each holiday on its own merit. I no longer wish to overrun one holiday in anticipation of the next. Enjoy the journey. We are always in a rush to get to the next big thing. Why not stop and enjoy all of the other things along the way?

Cod Dinner

I am having cod for dinner. Having cod for dinner with Fuzz-butt in the house is a challenge. He sits there and gives me the guilt look. You know the one. It is the same look a woman gives a man when she feels that he has not performed a chore satisfactorily. It is the look that makes a man drag his butt up off the couch and do it over, her way, even though his way was obviously the more logical solution. Fuzzbutt does that too! He stares me down for fish. I give him some. He inhales it like a Great Dane with a hot dog and then he stares at me again. It makes my dinner so stressful! I have to choke down my meal in a hurry just to avoid the look! If I give him too much, he just keeps stuffing it in and then goes and throws up in my shoes or something. If I lock him in another room, he calls PetSmart and reports me for abuse! I don't know why he thinks that PetSmart cares, but it is embarrassing for me when I go in there. Then they are watching me to see if I buy the cheap cat food and non-organic catnip. Maybe I should just become a vegetarian.

Naomi

Her name was Naomi and she was in her sweatpants and t-shirt relaxing at the coffee shop when I arrived. We talked about the usual things, growing up, family, work, goals. I then asked her why she thought she had never been married.

"Well?" she said chuckling. "I was crazy, madly, deeply, head over heals for one guy. He was good looking and outgoing. He had a wonderful sense of humor. He had a nice family. His mom even liked me! I could not ever figure out that no matter how hard I tried, no matter how much I bent over backward, nothing I did seemed to inspire him to feel the same way! He told me he thought I was a great person, but in the end, I just lost him without a good reason. This really bothered me for a long time."

Naomi went on to explain about how she would go on the occasional date or be "fixed up" from time to time, but that these were all just very uninspired encounters that simply never developed into any sort of relationship. She was happy. She had friends and a cat (laughing)! Overall, her life was good. She simply kept moving.

"That relationship! Sure, I got over it, but it bothered me for years just trying to figure out what I had done wrong! He had been kind of a big deal to me!" she continued. "Then, a couple of years ago, I met someone new. A very nice, professional, caring guy. We hit it off quite well. He was not necessarily my usual 'type', but he had so many good qualities that I simply could not overlook him. It was a very good relationship. People saw big things in our future together. But, the longer we were together, I began simply to feel uninspired. Nothing at all against him. It was all on me. And then, it hit me. This was a mirror image of the relationship that had bugged the crap out of me for ten years! I was now with a man who was crazy about me and doing anything and everything to please me! Yet, the more he did, the more annoying he became. I simply knew that he was not someone I wanted to spend my life with! Again, nothing against him, he was a great guy! But, now I found myself searching for a way to exit his life without hurting him. I really tried! But the more I pulled away, the harder he tried to make it work. I ended up hurting him just as I had been hurt all those years earlier and I am certain that he was standing there wondering what the heck he did wrong. The sad thing is that he did NOTHING wrong! Nothing. Sometimes, I think maybe I am better off staying single (smiles)! But then again I still have that image in my mind of this beautiful lifelong love affair that I sure hope is out there waiting for me somewhere!"

Naomi told me that she has not given up on love. She now feels that she understands better how to not smother someone you love as that can do nothing but make things worse. "If it is right, it is right. If it is wrong, it is better to find out sooner than later."

☞

Pain in the Butt

I had to go to the doctor's office the other day for a problematic hemorrhoid. He said, "Well, L.E. you are almost fifty-two and still haven't had a colonoscopy yet! We can send you to one guy who can fix both of those issues!"

Lucky me!

"They will band the offending blood vessels down there!" he continued as I turned pale. "After that, they will get you set up for your colonoscopy prep and procedure!"

The tone of his voice sounded as if I had won a Bahamas cruise or something, but the visions inside of my head suggested horror and agony. He is my ex-wife's doctor too! I also suspect he may like her better! Did she play a part in this? Are they in cahoots?

I did some research on this whole banding thing. They tie the vessels with rubber bands to cut off circulation so that they fall off in a week or two! Sometimes they even INJECT THE HEMOR-RHOID!!!!! I just know that Sally is behind this!

I spoke by phone today to the colon and rectal specialist's secretary. Who the heck wants to grow up to be that kind of doctor anyway? So, the woman on the phone proceeded to tell me that

I will need to come in for an initial consultation. She will email me forms to complete and bring along to the appointment. Then, she added one more item to my homework.

"You need to go to the drugstore and purchase a Fleet Enema and use it one hour before your appointment" she said smugly.

This evil witch must know Sally too! I have never had a need for an enema in my life! Why do I need to start now? I WANT MY MOMMY!

The appointment is next week. Please pray for me!

✳✳✳

I have my colon and rectal doctor's consultation appointment tomorrow. I filled out a bunch of paperwork online today in preparation. It was quite invasive. It asked about if my parents were still alive or how they died. It asked if my brother had ever had polyps removed. It also wanted to know if I would scream like a twelve-year-old girl if someone offered to ram a six foot hose up my butt. They wanted to know what medications I take and what surgeries I may have had and if I would object to wearing a maxi pad after hemorrhoid removal. They wanted to know about how close I live to the clinic, my drinking and smoking habits and my emergency contacts so I listed Detective Olivia Benson at SVU.

Dr. Varun

I had my rectal consultation today for hemorrhoids and colon screening. I went there and completed some papers. I then spoke with a pleasant woman who took my blood pressure. Then things turned mean and nasty when she told me how much I weighed. I threatened to lay a smackdown on her for saying such things! I think she took offense because she then took me to an office and left me. I waited there for quite some time for Dr. Varun. He came in all smiles asking me what brought me in today. I explained that my regular doctor thought it was time for me to have a colonoscopy and to have my butt checked. He smiled again and then started texting.

I peeked. "Honey, go ahead and place an order for that new hardwood flooring in the dining room." it read.

Why would he be talking about that in the middle of my meeting? What could have possibly made him think about floors at a time like this?

Anyhow, he took a couple of notes and then said, "Let's step into the next room and have a look."

I felt like a call girl who had just found gainful employment. He took me through the door and told me to drop my drawers and bend over the table. He then proceeded to tell me about proper poop habits while he violated me with various instruments of torture. Did you know that you should have a bowel movement the consistency of toothpaste two to three times each day? The things you learn while somebody has their hand up your butt!

So, he finished his inspection and took me back to the office. He said I get the colonoscopy next month and maybe a laser treatment later. Woohoo! He then sent me to see another woman to get my game plan in order.

I immediately reported to this lady that Dr. Varun had assaulted me. She just smiled. She then told me about the horrors in my future. Nothing but clear liquids for a whole day before my procedure and then laxatives, more laxatives and finally more laxatives. Then, the next day they will put me to sleep and shove the hose up my butt. I can't wait. The laser thing is to burn and shrink offending tissue. I asked her if there would be any smoke involved. Again, she just smiled. I took that as a very unpleasant yes.

∗∗∗

I have been getting calls from the lady at the Colon and Rectal clinic. We keep missing each other on the phone, just leaving messages. She says she has a couple of questions prior to my scheduled procedure on Tuesday and she sounds way too damned perky about it! The last time I went to this place, everyone was smiling but me. I felt so violated. Surely this type of thing must be illegal. Well, this time they want to run a laser up my butt and play Space Invaders, shooting the offending blood vessels until they shrivel up and die. Minor discomfort they say. Minor discomfort my ass! I Googled it and this was the picture I was shown. That thing is as big as the hand and they want to stick it where? Next thing the Googled article mentioned was the word cauterize. Uh, the last time I had anything to cauterize that area, it was due to some bad Mexican food. I have no desire to repeat the experience.

They want to put me through all of this "minor discomfort", yet I have heard no mention of lollipops or ice cream or attractive visiting nurses, nothing. They expect to just send me home with my butt smoking while they collect a tidy sum of money and get to have all of the fun.

C Day

Well, today was the day. I had been scheduled to have this treatment before Christmas, but it needed to be postponed until January due to a minor scheduling issue. Yes, today was the day to get shot in the butt with a laser gun. This is apparently the new way to control internal hemorrhoids. They ram this big contraption in your butt about half a foot and then pretend to be Captain Kirk on an away mission shooting his laser pistol at Klingon invaders.

The appointment started out reasonably well. This cute, young nurse came and retrieved me from the waiting room and took me back to an exam room with a funny looking table. She chatted me up, asking a few questions. Then, she told me that she was going to step out of the room while I was to drop my drawers and assume the position across the table. She told me the doctor would be in shortly.

This is when is got weird. Suddenly Barry White music started filling the room and before I knew it the doctor appeared in the doorway, smiling and wearing a Starfleet uniform. He seemed to be enjoying this whole thing way too much. He reminded me of the giddiness I felt in 1980 when I was in possession of a roll of quarters, entering a game room with a Space Invaders machine.

He seemed to be an old pro at this as he wasted no time at violating me. I mean, Barry was barely into his second verse! Once the contraption was in place, I felt warm bursts and ever so slight stinging sensations as the doctor suddenly yelled out, "Scotty, divert all power to the forward phase cannons!" And before Barry could belt out his final chorus, the deed was done. I was left alone, spread across the table as the doctor exited the room smoking a cigarette.

Me? I felt so violated that I just went home and stood in the shower crying for an hour. I then got on the phone and called Ice T to file a report. He told me that there was nothing he could do and that I should maybe seek counseling. Actually, he suggested inpatient treatment at Bellevue. I think I will be okay. Just please don't ever play a Barry White song around me.

Hot Mom

I was working an area of town known to be a college-age hangout. The streets were lined with bars, pubs, cheap food and lots of young people. It was 2:00am and the area was teeming with activity. I picked up a rider looking for about a thirty minute ride to the ritzy northern suburbs. She was blonde, attractive, smartly dressed. She was also quite talkative.

"I came here tonight to meet up with my twenty-one-year-old cousin and her friends for a few drinks. I really felt old being here! I am twenty-seven and I felt like the oldest person in the place!" She lamented. "Can you believe not one guy even offered to buy me a shot? I mean, I may be getting little lines at the corner of my eyes, but I think I am still hot! Right?"

This was obviously stressing out the poor girl. She told me that she was married and soon they were planning to start a family.

"I want to be the hot mom, you know? I don't want to be just the average middle aged woman!" She confessed. "This really sucks! I am calling my friend, Lisa. I need to tell her. I haven't talked to her in ages! I mean, it's Saturday night, she should still be up, right?"

There was about a thirty second pause in her conversation as she fiddled with her phone. "Hey Lisa, it's Kaitlin! How are you girl? It's been forever! Uh, it's about 2:30 I think...oh were you asleep? Oh sorry, should I let you go? Oh, okay great! I tried Lisa first but didn't get her. I just had an awful night. I met my cousin and her friends at a bar and I felt sooo old! I didn't feel like they thought I was hot! Remember how everyone always thought I was hot? I don't ever want to be not hot. I want to be a hot mom. I want fifteen-year-old boys to look at me and say, she's hot! What? Oh yeah, you're right. I probably shouldn't say that out loud about fifteen-year-olds huh. But, it's true! I want to always be the hot wife and the hot mom!"

Can you say hot? This poor girl was having a crisis! She was, shall we say, a hot mess! The call eventually ended and she bid goodnight to Britney. She told me that she had not spoken to Britney in over a year. She was glad they got to catch up a bit. She then jumped back on the phone to reconnect with two more friends, only reaching their voicemails.

"They must still be out partying." She commented.

"Yes, who would be in bed at 3am?" I replied.

About this time, we reached our destination and Kaitlin popped out of the car and on her merry way.

The Wendy Contract

Wendy wants to meet me tonight to talk with me "face to face" about this possible dating thing we have been considering. It's good, yet kinda funny how this, at the moment, is almost a business arrangement. I have had to make certain there were no major professional ramifications, since we work in the same company. We have touched upon the potential impact at the office and there are still some details to be ironed out before the journey begins. Oh the things we learn from our younger, foolish days where we just jumped right into these things without planning!

So, anyhow, last night Wendy stopped our conversation abruptly on the phone saying she knew if we kept talking that we would get into areas she wants to talk about face to face. I completely understood and agreed. Even though I don't wait well, I thought what the heck? It will be fun inking the final details of our "dating contract" together. She doesn't realize yet that I am a ruthless negotiator and good at getting what I want in a business deal!

But, now it's 4am and I am laying here awake in my bed. No big deal, that just happens sometimes. It is a good time to think, to ponder. The trouble is that I got to thinking about what it could possibly be that Wendy needs to tell me face to face? Hmmmm... Now my curiosity is getting the best of me. Could it be something big? I have some possibilities that I want to run by you to see what you think.

1. Her given name at birth was Larry.
2. The last three people she dated mysteriously disappeared. An ex-army ranger boyfriend was a suspect but no charges have been filed.
3. She is never allowed to return to Maine for undisclosed reasons.
4. She is very interested, but if I ever wear my Mr. Rogers sweater in public again, the whole deal is off.
5. She wants me to know that we have much in common, but from now on she controls the car radio.
6. ....

I will need to keep working on my list. Who knew there was so much to think about?

I wrote this story a while back and it somehow got lost in the shuffle. Wendy has since come and gone from my life, but it is interesting to look back at this story now. In hindsight, I was only right about two of the five possibilities I listed!

Fir

Hi, my name is Frasier. I am a pine tree. I stand about seven feet tall and I live out on the far corner of my owner's property near the side road. I have a good life. My owner mows around me, keeps me trimmed and feeds me fertilizer regularly. I have to put up with the neighbor's dog peeing on me sometimes and there is a cat that hides in me sometimes waiting for birds. He never seems to catch any, but he keeps on trying.

It is early December and my owner has taken his family to the mall. They are Christmas shopping. I don't really know what that is, but the children seemed excited. What is bothering me is these two guys that keep driving up and down the road in a pickup truck and slowing down to look at me. I don't know what they are up to, but one said something about the right size and it would save forty bucks.

☝

The Cost to Live

Let's do a math problem together. I did a little research. The average price of rent for a one bedroom apartment in the Indianapolis area, where I currently live, is $659/month. The average monthly utility cost is $164/month. The average grocery bill for a single individual is $292/month. Gasoline for one car $180/month. Car Insurance (just liability), let's go cheap $70/month (that's the low end of average.)

Where are we? 659+164+292+180= $1295/month

At the minimum wage, $7.25/hour, working forty hours per week, this individual would gross $1160.00/month. I used a paycheck calculator available online to then calculate the take home pay. It gave me a net of $1023.48/month.

$1023.48 earned
$1295.00 basic living expenses

-$271.52 shortfall

This budget includes no entertainment, no discretionary money, no children, no pets, nothing.

Let's pick on WalMart for a minute. Nothing against WalMart. They are just an easy example to use, but there are countless companies just like them. The most recent fiscal year, their CEO earned $25,600,000.00. As a company, WalMart's NET, yes NET, earnings in most recent reporting for the previous year was $15,880,000,000. That's nearly sixteen billion, with-a-B, dollars.

I realize that there are opportunities for people to get an education and earn more money. America is the land of opportunity. But let's take an example. I had a friend who worked hard. He exceeded his expectations. His IQ was not terribly high. He could never have expanded his educational abilities. He was just a nice guy who worked hard. Minimum wage jobs were about the limit of his options. Did he work as hard or harder than most of us? I would bet yes. Should he be punished for his IQ? Should he have to struggle just to survive?

It is no wonder that people begin to look for a government handout. Is there abuse of the system? Yes. Does the minimum wage need to be raised to a living wage level? It seems obvious that the answer is yes. One person cannot live on a full time minimum wage. Not part time, no babies, no lazy spouse at home. No extra money for anything. Companies CAN afford it! There will be some that will say it will drive them out of business. But who is the voice for those who cannot even afford to pay the most basic expenses yet work full time? Who will speak up for them? Let's use some common sense and do what is right.

I'm Not Mary

My phone pinged. I was being summoned to pick up Mary. The given address was in a small strip mall at a little pub down at the very end. There was a slender young female, early twenties, standing outside staring at her phone. I pulled up next to her.

"Are you Mary?" I asked. "I am a driver and was sent here to pick up Mary"

The young woman approached my opened window, "No, I am not Mary. I am Samantha. I wish I could help you, but that's not me."

The woman then smiled and wandered back to the front door of the pub. She opened the door and tripped inside, getting her foot caught awkwardly in the closing door. She was in such a predicament that it required the assistance of the bartender to free her. I sat there for a moment lost in my amusement as Samantha disappeared into the bar. After a couple of minutes, I decided to send a text message to Mary to let her know that I had arrived and was waiting in the parking lot. It wasn't thirty seconds before Samantha reappeared exiting the bar again. This time she approached the passenger side of my car, opened the door and plopped down in the front seat.

"Hi, I am Mary. Sorry, I forgot," She said with a smile. "I want to go up Allisonville road. Sorry, I am really drunk."

Boy, you could have fooled me!

"I had a light go off in my head tonight and I decided that I am going to break up with my boyfriend." Samantha...er I mean Mary continued. "I am only twenty-two and I need to be free to be just me. I don't even care if he wants to keep the apartment. I will move. I just don't need a boyfriend right now. I am going up here to Larry's Bar. They are closed but I know a couple guys who work there. We are gonna chill out, have a few drinks and talk about how I can get out of this situation I am in."

There are so many possible comments I could make at this moment, but instead all I can say is hmmmm …

Dating History

I have not dated much in my life really. I dated a little in high school and shortly thereafter, I swore off dating for a large part of my twenties. This will help to explain why I didn't date for all those years. After these experiences, I was scared!

It all started with this cute girl I met at the fire hall. She was a cousin to my neighbor a few houses up the road. Amy Jefferson. She was clear from the other side of the county. But, I was just about to get my driver's license and this girl didn't have any preconceived notions about me like the ones I had grown up with. So, I did some sweet talking persuading of her parents and deceived them into thinking that I was a proper young gentleman. Amy's father didn't really buy it, but I think her mother decided I was worth giving the benefit of the doubt. So, Amy and I started to go to dinners and movies and bowling and such. One afternoon, I was going to see Amy and I took my best friend Curt along. Of course I wanted to show her off to him and make him jealous. Well, you see, Amy had an older sister. Amanda was about a year older. I had never paid much attention because I was too busy looking at Amy. But, Curt quickly decided that Amanda was to his liking. Before you knew it, we were best friends dating sisters and old man Jefferson was not a happy camper! We would go out as a foursome to various places and events as teenagers do and when we would return to the girls' house and pull into the driveway, that porch light would start flashing! That was the old man's signal for the girls to get their butts into the house pronto! Curt and I were his worst nightmare come true in his eyes!

As things turned out, a couple of months into this arrangement, Amanda came down with mononucleosis and ended up in the hospital. Well, I had spent good money on tickets to a rock-n-roll concert and Amy wasn't allowed to go, with her sister in the hospital and all. What was I to do? Hey I am a genius! I simply devised a plan to keep everybody happy! I secretly asked Emily Conners to go with me to the concert. It was innocent! Emily and I had been friends for a long time! I didn't want to create any problems with Amy either, so I thought it best to keep this part a secret. I did, however, need to make an appearance at the hospital to "pay my respects" to Amanda and the family. I could do this no problem. I was Ferris Bueller before there ever was a Ferris Bueller. I had this in the bag.

I picked up Emily and told her I needed to run by the hospital and run in for a minute because Curt's girlfriend was a patient. I told Emily she should probably wait in the car. I went up to the room on the third floor. In the room were Amanda, Amy, Curt and the girls' mom. I said my hellos and chatted for a minute. I then excused myself because I had several "things" I needed to get done. Amy offered to walk me to my car, but I convinced her to visit with her sick sister as I was in a bit of a hurry anyhow. I went down to the parking lot, got in the car and went on my merry way. End of story.

Shortly after I left the hospital, Amanda received another visitor. It was a cousin of hers whom I had met a time or two. As she entered, she saw Amanda, her mom and Curt. Amy was seated just around the corner and out of view.

This cousin as she entered said, "Hi everybody! I just saw Amy and her boyfriend pulling out of the parking lot as I pulled in!"

At that moment, Amy popped out from around the corner and spouted, "NO, you didn't!"

Poor Curt! He was now trapped in a room with four angry women with lots of questions. This was in the days before cell phones and so I had no idea that his life or mine was even in danger. I did not learn that until I returned home at 11:30 that night and my home phone was ringing. Who the heck could be calling at this late hour? Oh, it was Amy and I had some 'splainin' to do! Long story short, I actually talked my way out of it in a day's time. A nice card, some flowers, and dedicating a song to her and all was forgiven. I was such a natural charmer!

Later down the road came Lori. She was a beautiful, sweet, kind girl who had grown up part of her life in my local area and then she and her family moved away. She and the girl who lived next door, Jayne, had remained friends over the years. As luck would have it, Lori came to visit Jayne when I happened to be around! I was quick to notice that Lori had grown up in all of the right ways! Wow! Once again I used my charm to get a date. We went out a few times and we really hit it off! She went away to summer camp and for some unknown reason, I got it into my teenaged mind that she was looking for a husband! I had no basis for this fear, but I quickly broke off the relationship and I am still haunted by the fact that the poor girl probably wondered what the heck happened! I sure hope I get the chance to apologize to her someday!

Then there was the girl I met at the roller rink. She was quite
a looker! Gorgeous dark hair and eyes, cute as a button! We were
both probably eighteen at the time. I lived about fifteen miles west
of town and she lived about that far south. We discovered that we
both liked to dance. Each Friday night I would go pick her up
and we would go to this fancy disco place in the next town over.
It just always happened to be that she was available on Fridays
to see me! She always came to the car. I never met her parents.
We would just go out every Friday to go dancing for about two
months. We would talk on the phone some too, but she was long
distance, so we didn't get to do that too much.

For those of you who are younger, it used to be that if you were
calling more than about ten miles from your house, the phone
company would charge your parents' phone bill by the minute
for time spent on a call. They were none too happy when a three
hundred dollar phone bill came delivered by the mailman. They
were even less happy when you got to the mail first and hid that
bill and the next one that came was six hundred dollars and it
arrived while you were at school! Not that anything like that ever
happened to me of course!

So anyhow, I was really liking this roller rink girl. She was right
up my alley! At least until the night she told me she needed to tell
me something. We had just finished dancing and were sitting in
the parking lot in the car.

"I am not going to be able to see you anymore," she confessed.

"But why?" I asked in total shock.

"Um … you see I am engaged to be married in a few months,"
she continued.

As I backed up the car to leave in disbelief, I bumped into
another car and broke my taillight. I was driving my mom's car. I

looked at the other car and it looked fine. So, I left the scene of the accident with my soon to be ex-girlfriend and my broken heart. A couple of weeks later, my mom asked me if I knew anything about a broken taillight on her car, of course I told her I had no idea. Obviously she must have hit something or a rock flew up, I told her.

Obviously, me and roller rink girl were through. She had wedding plans to tend to. I always wondered how that marriage worked out.

I am sort of skipping through my history here a bit. I did have a few good relationships. I fell madly in love with Marcell for a while. Then there was the hyperactive cocktail waitress whose mother kept telling her she needed to hang onto me because I was quite a good catch! She had such a smart mother. Then came Kathy. Kathy was a singer. I got to know her and started dating her and actually used her to fill in to sing at a few shows my band performed. One evening we traveled to a show about an hour's drive away. I owned a full sized cargo van and it was full of musical equipment. Across the front sat Mitch, the bass player, Kathy's sister Lisa, Kathy, and me. We traveled to the show and performed four hours. Mitch decided that night that he REALLY liked Lisa. He even told me that he wanted me to drop him off at his house last so that he could try to talk to Lisa more. So, we were homeward bound down a dark lonely highway at three o'clock in the morning sitting four wide across the front of the van. It was then that I began to feel fingers on the back of my neck. As I drove, I took inventory. My hands were on the steering wheel, check! Kathy's hands were on her lap, check! Mitch did not have arms six feet long to reach my neck, check! Uh oh! Lisa was rubbing the neck of her sister's boyfriend! Mitch was mad when I decided to drop him off first, but hey I needed to know the truth! I just ended up very confused, especially when they introduced me to Carol, the third gorgeous sister! I bet you are wondering what happened then! Gosh darn it! I am out of time for this story!

Time to Celebrate

Okay folks! It is one week until Christmas! It is now time to get into the holiday swing of things! I kinda feel sorry for those of you who missed Thanksgiving because you were in such a rush to get to Christmas! You may now be growing tired of it and be ready to get it over with already. Me? I am just getting started. I am full of steam and ready to roll!

I like to take the holidays as they come. Enjoy each one on its own merits. I don't like to get them all balled together. I do feel that maybe there needs to be some spreading out of the holidays. After New Years, things get kinda barren. We have MLK Day and Valentine's Day, then President's Day. That's about it. The dead of winter would be a fabulous time for a big celebration! There should be a Snowman day, where everybody builds a snowman. There could even be a booming business trucking in snow to the southern states for the event. Do that one in January. Then maybe in February add a go to the beach day. For those of us in the beach-less, cold Midwest, we could have an indoor beach holiday even at places like Lucas Oil Stadium. The place is just sitting there empty after football season anyhow. Bring in sand and a wave pool and a band!

I am just so full of it! Great ideas that is....isn't that what you thought I meant?

Golden Arches

I had a few minutes to kill today between appointments, so I ran into a McDonalds to buy a drink. While standing in line, I got to thinking about how different the place is compared to when I was young. They used to have the sandwiches pre-made in a warmer behind the cashier in rows. There was always somebody keeping track of those and yelling back to an unseen cook. They would say things like "Down three Macs! Holding on two McChickens!" Why do I even remember that?

I think that now everything is still pre-made, but just slapped together as you order it. They have sort of hidden the operation, but there appear to be little trays in warmers full of burger patties and chicken breasts and they sort of run it down an assembly line when ordered.

The fry making doesn't appear to have changed much, but they have added this whole coffee station thing. I don't drink the bitter stuff. That's for old people. But, I see lots of customers with their frappe latte cappuccino mocha whatevers. I have no clue what all of that even means. It's just all bitter. If they would just leave out the coffee, then maybe it would be good.

I must say that I was, however, highly impressed by a woman in her forties that I met recently at a Starbucks who actually ordered coffee. Nothing else, just plain old coffee. I was surprised they even sold it that way anymore! If you are going to drink coffee, then drink coffee. If you need to cover up the taste with all of the other stuff, then just leave the coffee out of it, right? Am I right? Well, of course I am! Everybody needs my opinion!

I always get off on these tangents! Back to my story! I also can recall going into Burger King when you could actually see a flaming grill back in the kitchen. I have tried to look, but as best I can tell, that has now been replaced with a microwave. I wonder where they really cook the burgers now! Just my curiosity.

Oh, and that woman who ordered straight coffee at Starbucks? She was supposed to get back with me in a few days. That was at least two weeks ago! I hope the straight coffee didn't kill her! It may have been sitting there since the last time someone ordered a cup in 1993! Poor girl!

Old Friends

I picked up Nick from a place known for its great food, typical American fare. It's the sort of place where you could get a good burger and fries, or a Reuben with onion rings, or maybe Buffalo wings. Nick was carrying a doggie bag. He told me he was headed to the next town, about fifteen miles away, to meet a female friend of his. He explained that the two of them had known each other for about ten years and that she would call him once or twice a year wanting to get together.

"She had a date with some dude tonight, but I guess she sent him home so that she could see me". He shared. "I really don't know what's up, but I didn't have anything going on, so I told her that I would come by." His phone rang, "I'm on my way. No, no, no you lost your chance to go out because it's now 11:05. You said you would be free by 10:00! What? No way! It's way too late. Maybe I will just stop and get a bottle of wine to bring. Girl, you are such a pain in the ass! I guess. We can just go to that place up the street from your place if they are still open." The call then ended.

"Hey, is it okay if we just swing in and pick her up and then you drop us by a club just up a ways from her house?" He was talking to me now.

"Sure, that's fine. You just show me where you want to go."
I responded.

Nick and I then had a conversation about how women are
impossible to understand. I shared with him my years of wisdom
on the matter and explained that he will never understand them.
I then gave him some pointers which I cannot share here because
a woman might read them and that would be in violation of the
bro code. If a woman ever learned these things, she would share
them with all other women and then they would surely find a way
to use them against men.

Anyhow, we arrived at Gretchen's house. She was waiting in
the garage with the door open.

"I hope she's not drunk." Nick said just as she started toward
the car with a stagger. "Oh God, she is drunk. I'm sorry dude. She
won't ever shut up when she is drinking."

I assured him it was okay. We would manage as she slid into
the rear seat.

"Hi mister driver! You are cute in that sweater!" Gretchen
said smiling.

"What the heck happened with your date?" Nick inquired.

Gretchen got a look of disdain on her face. "This guy was
something else! We went out for drinks. We didn't even eat! All I
had was a bucket of beer and a few shots. When the bill came, he
didn't have enough money to pay for it! So, I just snatched up what
cash he had and put it on my credit card. What a loser! When we
got back to my house, I just sent him on home!"

"He didn't even feed you?" Nick reiterated.

"No! I am starving!" Gretchen replied.

We had arrived at their destination. They both hopped out
of the car and in they went. Another satisfied ride-sharing customer!

Rideshare Wisdom

I like to think of myself as religious due to the influence my grandmother had on my life. She tried to instill in me traditional beliefs. I consider myself a Christian, although I stopped going to church once I became an adult. I do believe in God. I also do believe in evolution. I think it is possible that both are real. I want to believe that there is a Heaven. I have lots of still unanswered questions in my mind on this subject.

Here is what I can tell you. If you are a good person and don't steal, hurt, murder, abuse, etc. … then I believe you should be able to go to Heaven. I do still drink and say bad words (smiles), but I try to generally be a good person.

Jean the Babysitter

I went to visit my babysitter recently. She basically took care of me all day, nine months out of the year, five days a week, until I was five-years-old. Jean was like an extra mother and her husband and kids were like an extra father and siblings to me. I was a lucky kid to be so loved. Most days, for most of the day, it was just Jean and me at her house. We did lots of fun things together. We baked cookies and made homemade doughnuts (I got to eat the warm doughnut holes). We also made lots of fresh breads and my personal all-time favorite, cinnamon rolls! A warm, freshly baked cinnamon roll from Jean's oven was the absolute best! The sweet and buttery smell would fill the kitchen with anticipation. The rolled-up, ooey-gooey, bubbling goodness coming out of the oven was almost more than I could stand. And I always had to make sure and stuff myself before the bigger kids got home from school, plus I just knew that Jean loved me the best! Since I was usually the only one home, I didn't have to burn my nose pressing it up to the oven window so that I could pick the best one before they came out. Nope, I could take my sweet time inspecting the batch for the prime, perfect rolls.

We did lots of other things too. We watched the soap operas. I guess that was more her thing than mine. I just kind of played while those were on. All of those people seemed so serious to a four-year-old. We also would go to Jean's father's house out in the country and help him and "Aunt Pearlie" with things. I really never knew where Aunt Pearlie fit into the equation. All I can recall is that she reminded me in stature and demeanor of Granny on the "Beverly Hillbillies" TV show. She was a feisty old gal. She had a very businesslike, no-messing-around attitude. I kept waiting for her to grab a gun out of the closet and go shoot some varmints.

Jean is probably responsible for me meeting my first real love interest too. Well, there was that other blonde haired chick from up the road, but she just liked to dance with me because she thought I was a girl, but that's a whole 'nuther story. Anyway, Jean was responsible for me meeting Shawna. She was maybe a year younger than me and I was sweet on her for a long time. We even got in trouble together one day at Jean's house for throwing rocks at cars as they drove by. Now if that ain't true love, then I don't know what is!

One of my most memorable moments from staying there, however, involved the butcher shop next door to Jean's house. On occasion, she and I would go over there for the day and she would help them cut meat. I usually just played around outside while she was there. It was usually boring. But, on this particular day, they had some chickens running around over there. Nobody had prepared me for this amazing sight I was about to see. The old man butcher came outside with an axe. One by one he would gather up a chicken and hold it on top of a stump and then WHACK! This is where the amazing part came in for a four-year-old. Jean and I had the job of chasing down these headless chickens as they ran around the parking lot. At that age, I thought this was the most amazing thing I had ever seen in my life! One of them even ran all the way down the bank to the creek before we caught up with him! I was too young to realize what a bad day this was for the chickens, but for me, it was one of the most incredible sights I had ever seen!

As I had mentioned, I went to see Jean recently. She is now an elderly woman. She is doing reasonably, well other than her eyesight is failing. We chatted and reminisced for a bit and it warmed my heart and probably hers too just to see each other again. I have not stayed in touch with her and others enough through the years. Life gets busy and before you know it, time is gone. I need to do a better job of letting people like Jean know how important they are to me.

Turkey Talk

Old women are gonna be the death of me. I had that whole incident with the one while Christmas shopping a few years ago, now today, there was one at the grocery store causing issues. Thanksgiving is coming up soon, so I wanted to get a turkey. I stopped by the market in order to pick up this and a few other items. When I got to the turkey freezer, you know, one of those open on top numbers for easy shopping, there was this old woman who had parked her ride-in Mart Kart and was now standing there hovering over the birds. She had the whole freezer blocked off as if she was afraid somebody else might get one before she had made her selection.

I muttered, "Excuse me," She ignored me.

"Nice selection of turkeys!" I continued, changing my tactics. She just glared at me momentarily.

I could see that she felt that I was nothing more than an annoyance to her day and she wanted me to just go away! Not a chance you old buzzard! I squeezed right in beside her and her cart, which she obviously didn't need in the first place! I jumped right in there and proceeded to pick up every single bird. Oh, I would stop occasionally and make a hacking coughing noise and scratch myself, but I made sure that I was in her way.

As I handled the turkeys, I made small talk, "I just love that new coating of snow we got last night don't you? My boyfriend was very sweet and went out and shoveled for me this morning."

She just had a look of disdain.

"He is one of those doctors without borders who have been working in Africa. He figured since we both already have AIDS, there wasn't any reason not to take the chance (cough, cough). Besides, he is an African American. Oh we make the cutest inter-racial couple you ever did see! Want to see a picture (reaching for my phone)? Ma'am, you forgot to get your turkey! Do you want me to pick one out and bring it over to your cart? Ma'am, Ma'am! Wow, you can really run fast! Have a nice day!"

Dad Was a Vet

My dad was a veteran. He served during WWII. He would sometimes share stories with me. He talked mostly about the places he had been, France, Germany, even Iceland. I think Iceland fascinated him the most with the hot water running down the streams in this cold climate. He also talked about a few of the men with whom he served.

He rarely talked about the war itself-the fighting, the ugliness. He kept that to himself for the most part. I think he was protecting us from it. This ugliness got to him though. He had been through a nervous breakdown and suffered residual difficulties for the balance of his life. Today they would probably say he had PTSD.

Today, I will remember him. Actually, I remember him every day. But, today I will remember him for what he endured, for the horrific journey he made, for the fact that he made it home and ended up living a very good and long and happy life.

Thanks Dad, for your service to our country and for making it home alive to be the best dad a guy could ever ask for.

Dirty Laundry

On my most recent trip to Pennsylvania, Mom wanted to talk about washing clothes. At eighty-nine-years-old, she has seen many changes and for some reason she had this particular subject on her mind. She remembers as a young child, they used a washboard to scrub clothes clean. This was a very manual method that certainly would have created some women with big, muscular forearms. Personally, I would have been afraid of these women!

A great new invention came along not too long into Mom's early life. My grandparents bought a hand cranked washing machine! For this one, you only had to carry several buckets of water up the hill from the spring, unless you were lucky enough to have full rain barrels up near the house. This water had to then be heated and placed into the washer. Once loaded, you got to crank away until the clothes were clean. You would then run them through a manual wringer before hanging them on a clothesline to dry. Again, more women with big arm muscles!

The next step in the evolution of laundry cleaning was one which I had never heard of before. They stepped into the modern age with a gasoline powered washer. Yep, it had a motor like a lawnmower or garden tiller on it. This made doing the laundry a noisy, if less labor intensive endeavor. No more cranking! This model was also equipped with a clothes wringer right on the unit! This thing looked sort of like two hard rubber paint rollers between which an article of clothing would pass to remove any extra water and reduce drying time.

I always knew that the top knuckle on Mom's left index finger was very crooked, but I never knew why. Now I do! It turns out that this clothes wringer was the culprit. She once got her finger caught in the thing! It sure sounds painful! I wonder how many injuries were caused by this contraption. Of course Mom didn't go to the doctor and when her finger healed, it healed crooked. Made her hand look like she could be the wicked witch of the west!

As time went on, mom graduated to hauling her clothes to the local Laundromat. This was about the time that I came along. I recall spending many an afternoon running around getting into trouble out of boredom in that place. The whole neighborhood washed their clothes in the same machines. We never really thought twice about it. The biggest hassle was loading the car, heading to the Laundromat, and finding that the place was full of other customers. Then, you got to haul all the stuff home and try again later.

Eventually, Mom and Dad bought a washing machine and put it in the basement. But, this was a few years after I had moved away and was permanently scarred from the endless hours spent at the Laundromat. I think they are a dying breed, however. I know that I currently live in endless suburbia and I would need to drive several miles just to find a public laundry. Yes Mom, times have certainly changed.

Chinese? Food

Will had a birthday last week. In our family, it is common for the birthday boy or girl to pick a restaurant where they would like to go. This works great for everyone but me. One year I picked Skyline Chili and the whole family had a fit. But, it was MY birthday, right? I am still brooding over that one! Anyhow, much to nobody's surprise, Will wanted Chinese. The official family celebration got pushed back due to a funeral out of state, but, I still wanted to make his day special. So, I went and picked him up at college to go out.

Will wasn't sure which Chinese place was best in his small college town, so we Googled it. We chose a place with 4 1/2 stars out of 5. When we arrived, it appeared to be primarily a take-out joint but with a few tables inside. It was the kind of place where you proceed to the front counter to order. We were greeted there by a man with red hair pulled back in a ponytail and wearing a skull cap. His features didn't appear to be Chinese, but one of his many tattoos did have some Chinese writing in it. He took down our order and then yelled it back to a woman standing at the front of the kitchen. She appeared to be the person who bagged up to go orders and stuff. She did indeed appear to be Chinese. She was also the translator, who in turn yelled back the food order to the two cooks. Okay, so sounds authentic enough, right? The redhead yells in English back to the Chinese lady who then yells In Spanish back to the two Hispanic cooks. What is more authentic than that?

Kokona

My thoughts are with Kokona today. She is from Japan. She has been working diligently to finish a project here in Indiana so that she can make it home to see her father. He has been told he is terminally ill with only months to live. Her plan for these past few months has been to finish up her duties here by the first of December and then go back to Japan to spend time with her father and help her mother for his remaining days. Here it is November 11. Unfortunately, things have suddenly taken a negative turn. Her father is now in an intensive care unit connected to a machine to help his breathing. His daughter is in a rush to make it home, half a world away. It will take the better part of a day to get there. He has been told she is coming. He cannot speak, but he smiled. It is believed that he is waiting for his daughter. He is waiting to see her once again. I wish her a speedy and safe journey. I hope they get to have that moment that they both so desperately want.

Frog Cure

I have had a frog in my throat all morning. I don't feel like I am getting sick or anything, just couldn't seem to shake the hoarseness deep in my throat. I tried drinking something and taking a cough drop, nothing helped. I kept coughing and hacking, no luck. Finally I had to break down and bring out the big guns. Jambalaya. The cure for any congestion from which you may suffer. Now, to be honest, I cannot say that just any Jambalaya will do. All I know is that the Cajun place up the road from my house has the cure. Their version is not hot to the tongue like some foods may be, but it will make you perspire profusely out of every pore north of your shoulders. The mixture of rice and chicken and sausage and spices and the buttery garlic bread—yes, you have to have the bread. It doesn't do anything to help with the congestion, but it certainly is good for the soul.

When I go to this place, they bring me out a big platter of the stuff. I can be a big eater, but I only usually make it through about half of the plate. Why? Well, because by that time, my hair is soaking wet, my neck is soaked, my ears are sweating and even my eyelids are fully saturated. No, I am not kidding.

When it makes your eyeballs sweat, the congestion is gone. I then leave smiling, with open sinus passages, and run home to eat a few dozen antacid tablets. But, it's worth the trouble. The frog is gone!

Women's Rules

Is it just me? Or do women do strange stuff? I had contact with a woman the other day and she said she would be getting back to me in a day or two. That was like two weeks ago. I even sent her reminder text. It is as if she has fallen off of the earth. Women do stuff like that a lot. If I look back over the years, I can find lots of examples of bizarre behavior. I can think of a couple of times where in a social setting I met a woman for lunch or dinner or coffee or something, and we had a very nice time. It was obvious that they were enjoying my company. But yet if I tried to contact them again, it was like they had just disappeared. Gee, I hope they didn't run a background check on me!

Currently in both business and personal matters, I am waiting on responses from six people. These are various things that they are to get back to me on. As I think about it, five of these people are women! What's up with that?

Also, as I look back at my social life, over the years, I have gotten some widely varying reactions from women. Some of them look at me like I either smell bad or have a third eyeball or something, while others look at me like I am a piece of filet mignon perfectly prepared and they haven't eaten in three days. There is no rhyme or reason to which women fit in which category. They're kind of all over the map. I can give you an example. Way back in my 20s, there was this girl that work for the same company that I did. She seemed like a nice girl. She had a nice personality. She was also kind of cute. So I thought what the heck, I asked her for date. She said no! (The little wench) However, just a couple of weeks later, she asked my ugly friend to be her date to some wedding she had to go to! Again, what's up with that?.

Some people say that women like to play games. Oh I wish they would send me the rulebook. Perhaps they just invent the rules as they go! I bet that is it! They don't want men to know the rules! That's it! I am going to write a rulebook! I will give it to every woman I meet. That way the game will be fair! Problem solved! Wait a minute, what's this game called anyhow?

Lunch on Me

I went to Cracker Barrel for lunch the other day. Actually, I had pancakes and they were good, but that is beside the point. As I was finishing my meal, I saw a familiar face across the room at another table. It was a man I had known a few years ago but had not seen in awhile. He was eating lunch with his wife. I could see that they were nearly finished eating as well. An idea popped into my head!

When I got up to leave I made my way, undetected, past my old friend's table. Without breaking stride, I picked up his bill from his table and kept walking toward the door and the cashier. My friend stopped me before I paid with a smile on his face.

"You don't need to pay my bill!" he said.

"I know," I replied, "But, I want to."

We exchanged a couple more pleasantries. I then paid his bill and mine and was on my way. I really didn't think much more about it. However, later that day I received a text message.

"I just wanted to say thank you again for lunch! It was a bright spot in our day from doctor visits," he wrote.

"You're welcome, my friend. I hope your doctor's appointments were nothing too serious," I replied

"My wife has breast cancer." he continued. "She had surgery last week and we were scheduling chemo today. She is doing good. Surgery seems to have gotten everything, but still needing to take precautions."

Next, my phone rang. It was my friend. He went on to tell me that this whole ordeal started only a couple of weeks before, after his wife mentioned to the doctor about something that didn't seem right. The next thing they knew there were tests and surgery and now chemo … boom, boom, boom.

He explained how they have been keeping this quiet and not really sharing the news with many people. He also said that my little surprise had meant the world to them in the middle of a stressful day. I simply told him that I was happy to do it.

My act was small. Insignificant. Yet, in that exact moment, it was big to my friend and his wife. Something inside me simply pointed me in the right direction that day. I take no credit. I was merely the tool.

Drink Pics

I have noticed in recent times that frequently on texts and social media that people pose for pictures with an alcoholic beverage. "I am here unwinding from a hard day at work with my margarita" or "I am pairing some grilled pacific salmon with this fabulous craft ale". Why is that a common habit? Why is it only with alcohol?

Why do you never see someone with a captioned photo that says, "I am on vacation in Bermuda and relaxing by the pool with an exquisite can of Sprite and some pork rinds." or "This glass of tap water really compliments these organic turnip greens."?

I think that we like to say the eloquent names such as Stone Mint Chocolate Imperial Stout or Voodoo Doughnut Bacon Maple Ale. No I did not make those names up. Those are real beers. It used to be that there were just beers. Now they have gone upscale. There are Spring beers, Summer beers, Fall beers, Winter beers, sipping beers, fruit beers and wheat beers, just to name a few.

Then there are wines. This is where things REALLY get confusing. Quilceda Creek Columbia Valley Cabernet Sauvignon or perhaps Cune Rioja Imperial Gran Reserva 2004 is more your speed. What? How the heck does someone even know where to begin to make a selection? At least you sound sophisticated pronouncing the names.

I was impressed after doing a bit of research to discover that according to Wine Spectator Magazine that Hewitt Cabernet Sauvignon Rutherford 2010 was the fourth best wine of 2013. Interesting. I didn't know that anybody in the family was even growing grapes. I guess I need to check to see who has purple feet at the next family reunion. They must be doing okay. The article said this wine was $92 a bottle and that there were 2,592 cases made. So, then I looked up how many bottles are in a case. The answer is twelve. So 12 x 2592= 31,104 bottles x $92 = $2,861,568.00. Wowza! All of that money for sour grapes!

I think I am going to buck the trend and start posting pictures of me enjoying a plastic bottle of water or a paper cup of Hi-C Orange at McDonald's. I am just a rebel like that.

Thanks Alyssa

"I decided I needed to use rideshare today because I am from Arizona and I have never driven on slippery roads" Alyssa confessed.

I learned that she had come to Indiana to go to college, studying to be a pharmacist. She was in her second year and had taken a job at a drugstore about ten miles from campus as a pharmacy technician. It was her first day on the job. I happened to be her ride home.

"My feet and legs are really hurting, I am not accustomed to standing all day!" She continued. "In Arizona, I worked at a compounding pharmacy, but that was mostly sitting down mixing IV's and such".

We got into a typical conversation about how she liked the Midwest compared to back home. She talked about how she had never experienced anything close to the cold temperatures we get in winter. We also had a good laugh about how she thought they must be joking when the university told her before arriving that her dorm did not have air conditioning.

"In Arizona, that would be considered barbaric torture!" Alyssa smiled. "It still took some getting used to, the humidity and all.

Every part of my body would sweat, my drink would sweat, everything. But, I enjoy the change of seasons. I never understood this whole concept of Fall. It was fascinating to me to see the trees change colors and everything sort of transform. Back home, the cacti all pretty much look the same year round."

I had, from time to time in my life, run into people who had never seen snow. But, for someone to talk about how they did not understand the concept of a fall and the leaves turning vibrant oranges, yellows, and reds, that really struck me. I have always felt that a tree lit up in vibrant crimson is just about the most beautiful sight in all of nature, yet we take for granted what many people throughout the world have never seen, nor do they understand what they are missing. Sure, they have probably seen pictures. But, a photo without those scents and sensations of the crisp air amid the still warm sunshine cannot be adequately described without being there.

Thanks Alyssa, you gave me a renewed perspective without even realizing it.

✳✳✳

I find some of the oddest things in the mail these days. I keep getting lots of mail for a former significant other. One today was a postcard inviting her to a church ice cream social. It said if she came and brought the postcard that she would get a free gift. What about me? I would like ice cream and a free gift!

Another envelope from another church stated on the front, "Two things that will lead to your miracle"

Why is she the one getting the miracle? I think she already had a miracle when she had me, right?

A Date with Dale

I had a date last Saturday night, with Dale. I found myself in possession of two tickets to a play, "The Odd Couple" and I needed someone to go with me. So, I called Dale. He is just slightly older than me, a nice guy, quirky, loves race cars and airplanes, and doesn't get out enough. I am not gay and neither is Dale and I told him when I asked him to go with me that he was certainly the ugliest date I had ever had and that there would be no goodnight kiss. Guys can say things like that to each other and laugh about it.

They play was great, well done, very entertaining. I even sat next to some people from Tennessee, who live very close to where I lived for many years. It was fun to reminisce with them. Dale also enjoyed telling them all about airplanes. The man had retired from the Air Force Intelligence Division and enjoyed racecars even though they stated quite clearly that they were not fans. But they seemed to enjoy his enthusiasm about the subject.

The surprise of the evening was that the star of the show was a pickle, yes a lowly pickle spear. If you know anything about the Odd Couple from movies or the old TV show, then you know that Oscar was a slob and Felix was a neat freak with odd habits. Well, in the play, Felix had made the food for poker night. Maury, the cop who is Oscar's friend, was raving over the sandwich that Felix had made him to another friend seated next to him. He even offered to share his pickle spear. Oscar was annoyed by this and reached over to smack the plate out of Maury's hand. Oscar hit the plate at such a perfect angle that the pickle flew up high into the air. It rose above the stage and then above the crowd before coming down and smacking some rather large, sophisticated looking lady square in the face in the third row.

What happened next reminded me of the old Carol Burnett Show when the actors would be trying to keep from laughing. The play basically stopped. The five men on stage stared out at the woman as if they were frozen. Then, one by one they began to jiggle as they attempted to hold in their laughter. The flustered woman did the only thing she could think of to do, a perfect response. She threw the pickle back at them. Oscar caught the pickle with a one handed stab. Maury quickly stole the pickle from Oscar and consumed the evidence. It was a priceless ad lib in a very good show.

Coming Home

Tonight I am in Pennsylvania, the state where I was born. I am sitting in the dining room of the house in which I spent my entire childhood. Beside me is a natural gas wall heater. This more modern version actually took the place of one of my favorite childhood memories. In that same spot, there used to sit a natural gas floor heater that operated on an internal thermostat and had a powerful fan forced blower built in. This heater was probably three feet tall by two feet wide. The flame was enclosed deep inside like a furnace. The front was louvered by horizontal metal slats that sort of resembled window blinds. I recall many cold winter nights bringing out a blanket, laying on the floor in front of this heater and propping my feet up on its face. I would wait with anticipation for the thermostat to click, the heating elements to warm and then the beautiful heat to blow filling my blanket with absolute heaven. It sends a chill up my spine just to think about it!

Now, I am looking up at the wall above the heater. There hangs an elementary school newspaper I brought home in 1971. I think I need to explain. About once a month, we students would receive this newspaper full of stories interesting to nine-year-olds. It usually had a crossword puzzle and a joke or two as well. It was not a locally produced paper from my school, but more of a national nature. This particular edition was special. If you completely unfolded it, on the back was a two foot by three foot calendar titled "You And Your Life." Basically, this thing shows all of the fourteen possible calendars that you can have and then there is a chart where you can look up which calendar to use for a particular year. This thing fascinated me, so my dad hung it up. Eventually, he even made a handmade frame for it. For a piece of newspaper, it is in fairly good shape. There is a slight watermark along the bottom from something that must have happened along the way. Also, if you look closely, you will see a slight ink mark on it. This mark happened before it was ever framed. It was me and my nine-year-old mind calculating something. What was I calculating? Well, I had read a story about average life expectancy... It might have even been in this newspaper. So, I decided to calculate from that information the exact date I was supposed to die. Yep! It's on there! No I do not recall the date nor do I wish to look as that day might be getting too close for comfort now!

On the opposite wall hangs Grandma Hewitt. Not literally! What hangs there is a very lifelike oil painting of her done by my cousin, Sam. He painted it as a gift to my father. It depicts my grandma sitting in a wooden rocking chair in a blue flowered sundress and an apron. She is peeling a bowl of potatoes. The painting is such a perfect likeness of her. It has hung there for probably thirty years now and is admired and cherished by everyone who knew her. She passed away when I was probably thirteen, but I spent many days with her playing dominoes and the fox and the hens and war and go fish and she always had those pink candy lozenges that taste like Pepto-Bismol. I loved those things! Oh and those orange circus peanuts too! Grandma was the best!

It is amazing, the memories just in this one room. I see a painting of an owl sitting in a moonlit tree done on what appears to be a piece of black slate. This was a gift from Mrs. Branch who lived up on the ridge right where you started out toward my Pap's farm. There is a real workhorse harness that was actually used on our farm that my dad mounted on a wooden base on the wall as you head toward the living room. I see a picture of my oldest nephew, Nathan, when he was about three. He is now in his thirties and old and ugly like the rest of us. Beside that is a collage created by my other nephew, Lee. It contains photos of him, his wife, their new baby, and several of my mom's favorite pets over the past few years. They made this for my mom the cheer her up when she was under the weather.

The final thing of note in this room is my mother's bowed glass antique china cabinet filled with dishes she has inherited from my grandmother and great grandmother. It means much to my mom. To me it was always a cause of stress. I heard the same words over and over during my childhood and even occasionally today, in my fifties, "Be careful! Watch the china cabinet! If you break that glass we will never be able to get a replacement!"

I haven't broken it yet, but you never know! I may just take off running through the house playing ball at any moment now!

I have now moved on to the kitchen. This kitchen is not the same one as the one in my earliest childhood memories. I was born in 1962. The kitchen was fully remodeled in the latest styles in 1971. It still is decorated in those modern 1971 styles today, 2014, Dreamscicle orange countertops and all! The gas range is from that same year. The refrigerator was replaced in about 1986. Oh, and let's not forget the microwave. It was a Christmas gift to Mom in 1981. It still works and if you eat something cooked in it and then go to the bathroom late at night in the dark, you can see a beautiful glow emanating from the toilet bowl. Mom does not believe in replacing something that still works, even if it does cause cancer and sterility.

Allow me to digress (wow, what a fancy word and I found a place to use it). Off the kitchen is a door to the back porch. Just off of the back porch is a fairly steep hill. To climb this hill, it is probably fifteen feet in which you gain ten feet in elevation. Then you reach a sort of shelf area that is relatively flat. This shelf area was where I often played as a child. I had a swing in a willow tree there and there was even enough room to play catch or a game of football. This is also the location where my earliest childhood memory began.

I was standing at the top of the bank when, suddenly, I had what I could best describe as an awakening. I paused to take in the world around me. I then laid on the ground and rolled all the way down the hill. When I reached the porch, I popped up, trotted in through the back door and into the kitchen where Mom was standing at the sink washing dishes.

I walked up to her, tugged on her pant-leg and said, "It's okay Mom! I am alive now!"

Without skipping a beat, she answered my profound statement, "That's nice. Now go outside and play."

I was very satisfied and proud of myself for making her aware of this big news. I merrily went on my way and quite honestly, I can recall most moments of significance from that point forward. I cannot explain it or assign it any particular meaning. That was simply my experience.

Okay, digression over. Now, back to the kitchen, this kitchen carries so many memories. It was the place where the fork got stuck in my head as I explained in detail in one of my earlier books. Also, in a home without air-conditioning, this was a brutal place to be when mom needed to bake a cake in July. It was also the place where I could stop in during my lunch break from a job I had early in my adulthood and Dad would have homemade potato soup and cornbread waiting for me on a cold winter's day. It is the place where Curt and I would get yelled at for spinning on the barstools while playing Yahtzee or some board game. We were always told we were going to break those barstools! Um, fortysomething years later, those barstools are still here. I think Dad lied to us!

I have now relocated myself to my bedroom in the house that built me. My parents, over the years, turned it into a storage room for junk and cluttered it up. How dare they! Many things here, however, are still mine. The desk is the same one I stored all of my good stuff in and where I sat pretending to do my homework. That picture of the monkey on the wall is mine. Also, the big sombrero is mine. Good to see they kept some of the important stuff. The dark paneling was my choice and the salt and pepper shag carpet was my idea too! I was amazingly cool and needed a room to reflect that. In one corner sits a full leg cast. My father broke his leg probably twenty years ago and for some reason they chose to keep the cast. He passed away about nine years ago, but his cast is still here.

This room is where I became a drummer and where I penned my first original song. It is where I learned to play the guitar, sore fingers and all. It is where I laid awake and laughed or cried as a result of the trials and triumphs of growing up. So many memories can be tied to this little ten by twelve foot room.

Why have I been writing about this old house? Well, soon I won't be able to sit here amongst this history and reminisce. As I mentioned, Dad is gone. Mom is eighty-nine-years-old and having mobility issues. Mentally she is great, but her walking is very labored. Therefore, she can no longer stay here safely and has moved to an assisted living place. We have come to the decision to sell the house and we do have a buyer. This buyer is willing to take the house 'as is', cats and all. Mom has both indoor and feral cats, so that's a big deal to her. The other great thing is that the buyer is not in a hurry to occupy, so we have ten months to pack up and sort through sixty years of accumulated stuff. Change can be bittersweet, but I am happy that I get the chance to say a long good-bye to what will always be my home. I know every nook and cranny of this place and I will take the time to rediscover many of those details before the time comes for my final good-bye.

Conversations with Mom

Mom called me on the phone today. We had our usual conversations about the weather and people who died that I should know but don't remember. There was also the conversation about Ray Gallagher's sister's aunt's cousin, from her second marriage, whose parents got some oil and gas money up on Hopewell Ridge and so they "helped" their daughter buy a house just up past the feed mill on the left. You know, the one with green shutters. Sorry Mom, I have no clue regarding who or what you are talking about. I moved away thirty years ago.

So, next subject was money, Mom's money. She told me that if she lives too long that she will end up spending Charles' and my inheritance. I told her not to worry. We will figure out something. Since the conversation, I have been brainstorming ideas before I call Charles. Perhaps I could arrange for Mom to accidentally fall out of the car while doing seventy on the interstate on our way back from having chili dogs and fries with gravy. I wouldn't want that to happen on the way there and miss lunch, but middle of the afternoon would work. Charles has been doing that whole preaching thing. Maybe he could arrange a baptismal malfunction.

I am sure Mom has some sins that need cleansing. The one driveway at Mom's house goes up a steep hill. I am always telling her to take a joyride in her wheelchair and I will pick her up down by the road. If I timed it just wrong, there might accidentally be a big dump truck coming around the bend when she got down there. See Mom, there is no need to worry about you spending our inheritance!

Finally, Mom must have been blabbing too much at the assisted living place, because, the Activity Director contacted me, asking if I could come and play and sing for the residents. I told her that I would be willing to do that, but they need to supply event security in case anybody gets out of control and starts throwing Depends on stage. She agreed and said she would initiate crowd control measures. Well, now, today, Mom is concerned about what songs I am going to perform. She was asking me if I was going to do songs I wrote and some old songs that the people she hangs out with might know. No Mom, I thought I would do some "Uptown Funk" and maybe some Eminem for them followed by Skynyrd. She then told me that I had better be working on my voice some before then, because I probably don't sound so good anymore. Gee thanks Mom! What would I do without you to cheer me on?

Trouble

I sometimes get myself into trouble. Well, okay, it actually happens more often than I would care to admit. I really, honestly don't intend to, it just happens that way. For instance, the other day, I made a sarcastic comment on a close friend's Facebook page. Some other friend of theirs thought I was being a bully and told me off right then and there. I thought my comment was funny. My friend thought it was funny. This other person wanted me strung up by my evil tongue!

Then, yesterday, I was just texting and driving, minding my own business doing about 30mph in a 40 zone. This guy got right up on my bumper as if we were running at Daytona International Speedway. I tried to be polite and just tap my brake lights to get him to ease off a bit. This tactic had no effect. I then slowed up a bit so that he could pass me. But he still remained halfway up my tailpipe. So, I decided that it would be fun to give him a true NASCAR racing experience. I pretended that there was an accident happening right in front of me and I hit my brakes really hard! I then just sat there. After collecting all of his belongings off of his front windshield, he proceeded to go on by me. He even honked at me in appreciation as he passed.

Fifty-Two

Another birthday is here! Fifty-two and counting. When my father was fifty-two, he was old in my eyes. Active but old. Me? I don't feel old and I certainly don't look any less handsome than I did thirty years ago! Along with that, I still act like I am ten. I still play. It just hurts a little more. I still run and jump and … well, Donald, Elizabeth's boyfriend makes fun of how I run. His imitation looks kinda like Forest Gump running away from those boys who were chasing him. Personally, I think I run more like Usain Bolt, the Olympic sprinter. Donald is probably just jealous.

I still have hair! That's a big deal! Many of my childhood friends, I won't mention names but they know who they are, have gone partly to mostly bald. I have even added hair in extra places, like my ears! That's my spare hair just in case I need it later.

I am forever honored to be a Halloween baby. I love that my special day is a day of celebration and fun. Heck, on the day I was born, my dad had to hurry home to take my older brother, Charles, Trick or Treating. He may have gained a brother, but he saw that as no reason to miss out on all of the Halloween booty!

So, however you are celebrating my birthday, have fun and be safe tonight. And if you haven't sent my gift yet, get on the ball!

☝

Perfection

Perfection. Some of us believe that perfection is what we should strive for in life. But, as humans, we are never gonna be anywhere near perfection for very long. We always find a way to screw things up. The best we can do is to learn to laugh at our shortcomings. Or should I say everybody else's shortcomings, because, of course, I have none!

It has never been my fault when keys or remotes come up missing. Somebody is simply playing tricks on me. I ALWAYS put things back where they belong. It's those damned kids! I also always finish what I have started without any interruptions or sidetracks. I never forget something in the oven and burn it. I am cooking right now and fully aware of what time it will be done.

My diet is perfect. My body is chiseled perfection. Six pack? Yep I have one! I simply keep it padded for protection. I never forget to shave. If I have a scruffy beard it is always by choice. Those two mismatched brown socks the other day? My choice. A fashion statement. The bleach stain on my favorite sweatshirt? A beauty mark.

I know the world is all jealous. I know that it all revolves around me. It's ok. I know that I am the center of the universe.

Take my hair. It's not graying. It's distinguishing itself. I don't lose games at racquetball; I feel sorry for my opponents and permit them to win. I have never said a mean thing in my life. I have never done anything selfish. I won't ever grow old and feeble or lose my perfect, sharp memory. My mind is like sharpened surgical steel.

.....what's that smell? It smells like something is....oh crap! Hang on!

Sorry about that! I need to go. Will and I are going out to eat tonight because I am a PERFECT DAD!

On Fire

I have been on fire today! I have been super industrious (please hold your applause until the end)! I got out of bed. I ate toast with tea for breakfast. I got to use my new toaster. My birthday was a couple of weeks ago and when asked what gift I wanted, I said a new toaster. My only qualification was that it had to be able to accommodate wide bread. I try to eat healthier, whole grain breads and some idiotic companies still make toasters that only fit the narrower bread. Therefore, I would have to toast one side then flip it over and toast the other side, but by then the first side is cold. Who wants cold toast? Will bought me my toaster and he got one that takes wide bread, so now he is my favorite child. I heard that he fought for the right to be the one getting the toaster because it was a cheap and easy gift. That's my boy!

Anyhow, back to being industrious. I had some pending paperwork that needed to be completed. I know that most people are like me and hate filling out forms. There were four different sets and a total of seventeen pages to be completed. Have you ever noticed that frequently these forms will ask for the same information on several different pages? Doctor's office forms are the worst …

well and the government. They will have three or four different places for you to put your address or your insurance information etc... They probably hate me because I have just started putting, "see page one" or "see Melinda at front desk. I gave her the cards". Why do they want me to do their paperwork for them without putting me on the payroll? Doesn't my time have value?

Yes, industrious... I also had some revisions for my next book. The editor had sent me back some page proofs for review and I had to make a few minor adjustments. She said I couldn't call Congress one big *^%&^%##@# in published material without possibly mysteriously disappearing. She also suggested that I not refer to my ex as #@%&^%. She mentioned the possibility of litigation and such. So, I got that finished and scanned back to the publisher.

I fixed my lunch, a chicken burger and fresh cucumbers, yum! Not so much the chicken burger, but I love cucumbers, the skinny English ones, no seeds to put up with. I then sat and scratched for a bit. It is a man's primal right to just do some therapeutic scratching from time to time. I scratched my belly and my armpits and my neck and my butt. I felt much better afterward. Now, it is almost 3:00pm and I have two lengthy emails to write. I need to wash dishes and start a load of laundry. I may then got outside and shoot some basketball. Man, I am overworked!

Phone Blues

It is no wonder there are so many looney people in this world. I may have just joined them today. I have a simple problem. Elizabeth dropped her iPhone and the screen is covered in cracks. I thought, no big deal, I will give her mine and I have a spare older version iPhone that works great that is good enough for me. It was left behind from when one of the kids just had to have the latest, greatest upgrade a few years ago. It has actually been handy having a spare. I let a coworker use it for a while when they needed one and Wendy actually even used it for a few months when her own phone died. It has always worked great.

Elizabeth's boyfriend, Donald, attempted to reset this spare phone. When he went to restart it, it asked for an iTunes user name and password. We tried every one we knew, no luck. The last person to actively use the phone was Wendy, my ex-girlfriend. It is so lovely to need to contact an ex about these types of things. She shared her user ID and password. We tried that; no luck. We were at a loss.

Today, I decided it was time to get this issue resolved! Donald had tried Wendy's ID before, but I figured that he surely isn't as smart as me, so today I tried, no luck! So, I got on the phone and called Apple to explain my dilemma and seek results. I spent one hour and fifteen minutes on the phone with a very nice rep just so that they could transfer me to their boss. This boss got the phone unhitched from Wendy's account, but said I need to prove that I was the original purchaser of the phone. What? Like, I would have the receipt from 2009 or 2010, are you kidding me? He said I would need that to send to them so that they would feel comfortable about unlocking MY phone that has zero information on it. He also told me that if I call Sprint, my phone carrier, that they could whip me over a receipt by email lickety-split. I got his contact info just in case.

I called Sprint. The first lady asked me what the problem was so that she could connect me to somebody that could help me. I want her job. "Oh, I don't solve anything, but you still need to tell me your whole story and then tell it again to the next person too." She transferred me to a man.

The man quickly said, "I can resolve your problem. I just sent you an email with the info."

I told him to hold on. I checked my email. He had sent me the receipt for the most recent phone we had purchased, not the one from four years ago! I re-explained to him what I needed. He searched for another thirty minutes before telling me I need to go to the same location that I purchased the phone, because he doesn't show it in his records, but they can give it to me lickety-split.

Lickety-split my butt! That location no longer even exists! So tomorrow, I get to do this all over again! My question is this, "Why can't Apple and Sprint just talk to each other, rather than use me as the UNPAID middle man?" To me, that would be true customer service!

✳✳✳

I play a game like Scrabble on my phone against random people. One person, who I have never met, has played me for years now. We sometimes chat a bit. Just small talk.

Today she sent me a message. "I need a sugar daddy"

"Well, if your name is Rachel McAdams, then I am your man!" I replied

It wasn't thirty seconds until her screen name was changed to Rachel McAdams. Thanks for a great laugh, my friend.

Now, as for the REAL Rachel McAdams, I AM available, single, unattached and waiting for you to come and sweep me away! Those Hollywood Hunks are NOTHING like me, I promise!

Free TP

I received an email today entitled
"FREE BATHROOM SAMPLES".

My curiosity got the best of me. I opened the mail.

"CONGRATULATIONS! Free Charmin Samples Are Waiting for you.

Below this was a clickable link

"Get your toilet paper*"

I then checked out the asterisk meaning below.

"*supplies are limited".

By golly I had better hurry before I miss out!

No I did not click on the link. I did check the closet and my toilet paper supply is sufficient for the moment.

I also went ahead and read the fine print.

"Not associated with Proctor & Gamble"

I am assuming they are who actually makes Charmin. So if these people, who are giving it away, are not the ones who make it and are not affiliated with them, then why are they giving it away? Makes me go hmmm. I just knew it was too good to be true! I have dreamed about free toilet paper all my life but it just isn't meant to be.

Social Media Responses

Don't you just love some of the posts people put on Facebook? Political, religious, mundane, partial stories, hate posts (some people hate everything), love posts (some people love everything), pictures of the exact same thing 43,917 times, posts that require a response to confirm that everybody is still their friend, this is my song! (Actually it is their 794th song.). Don't get me wrong. There are some quality things on Facebook, i.e. everything that I post! It is also a great way to reconnect and stay connected with friends and family. It does, however, require just a bit of political correctness. Below are some sample posts and the responses I so badly wish I could give.

Post: Rushing out the door to the emergency room!

That's the entire post. Are they begging for people to ask why? If it is a true emergency, then I hope nobody died due to the time it took to post the Facebook status.

My Response: Oh Awesome!

I recall a post from someone just out of the hospital complaining because home health care services were not coming until the next day. The next day there was a post from the same person that they were at a steak and ribs place for dinner enjoying a glass of wine. You cannot make this stuff up!

Post: I just got home from WalMart. Meatloaf, mashed potatoes and corn is what I am making for dinner tonight

No special occasion or special meal. No crown rack of ribs or a birthday party-just meatloaf on a Tuesday.

My Response: I just took a healthy, relaxing forty minute shit before sitting down to a hot can of Spaghetto's

I love the shopping ones. Went to Target, bought some bath towels and a toaster, but they were out of Larry's favorite boxer briefs, so had to swing into Family Dollar for those.

Post: Some people need to just stay out of my business!

These nonspecific personal attacks against some unnamed evil person are supposed to do what?

My Response: You must be talking about (insert first name of someone from their friends list). You said he was nothing but a scumbag. Of course you also said that (insert another name from their friends list) is a real b*#ch and cannot be trusted! Which one is it?

Let's help get some real action going here!

Post: Oh here is another picture of my darling grandson Leroy! He turned 1 year 2 months 19 days and seven hours old just before this was taken! Isn't he just perfect?

Sharing a picture every now and then is great, but there needs to be a legal limit.

My Response: Oh yes, he is just adorable until he shits his pants!

They are babies. They are fun, but your baby is no better than all of the other hundred million babies out there. And we don't need to see them every day.

Now on to posts I would like to make on my own on Facebook!

Post: Does anybody know how to get human blood stains out of carpet in the car trunk?

Post: Hey (pick the random name from the friends list of a friend), I found a necklace in the parking lot when we were leaving the alcoholics anonymous meeting. I thought it might be yours.

Post: My Asian friends are looking for some stray animals to "adopt" if you know of any. (Now, before you send me hate mail, I have Asian friends and they would find this funny.)

Post: Shirley, I checked with the drugstore and they said that you do need to go to the doctor for those warts. They could be highly contagious.

Post: Just sittin' here, scratchin' myself and thinking 'bout you

Post: NO Renee! I will NOT marry you!

Post: Don't make me "out" you!

Post: Hey Jim, I left those detonators in your garage. What are you planning to do with all of that bomb-making material anyhow?

Facebook could be so much more fun!

Swipe Right

I love when I encounter some new phenomena of which I was totally unaware! Such was the case of three guys on a ridesharing trip the other day. They were talking about Tinder. To tell you how much I knew, I couldn't tell if they were saying Tinder or Timber. Anyway, here is how the whole conversation started.

"You should really come tomorrow night and meet Melissa." said guy one. "She is really sweet and has a good personality."

"Uh" chimed guy two, "Any time you start off by describing a chick you want me to meet by saying she is sweet and has a good personality, it makes me worry just how ugly she really is!"

"She's not that bad!" responded guy one.

Guy three then jumped in, "Is she a left swipe or a right swipe? On Tinder!"

Guy one was now on the spot. "Well, her best friend, Cindy is definitely a right swipe! But, Melissa? I don't know....probably a left swipe, but she is a great girl!"

I wanted to understand this girl swipe thing, so I went home and did my research! It turns out that on this website you post a picture. You are then given groups of pictures to look through each time you log in. In an instant, you swipe the picture with your finger, left for no and right for yes. If any of your yes swipes also swipe you as a yes, then they arrange a chat. Wow! Just weed through women based solely on looks by the hundreds at a time! I am betting a guy designed this app! He is so smart! Uh, unless you are a woman reading this story. If that's the case then, how stupid! Basing the start of a relationship on a picture! How dare they?

My research also found some other interesting tidbits. I found one young woman complaining that her Tinder photos always get removed as being too racy. I tried to contact her to send those photos to me so that I could give my unbiased opinion, but I could not reach her. I also read about a girl who was highly upset when her Tinder date went to "the bathroom" only to text her saying he really wasn't that into her. He also left her with the bar bill. There was also the girl who was seen having three Tinder dates at the same bar in one night. She would get one out the door with some lame excuse before the next one arrived.

We didn't have anything like this when I was in my twenties. I would have to trot my butt up to a woman, ask her out on a date, stand there while she laughed at me and then trot my butt back where I came from. Finally, after about a hundred rejections, I would come across a blind one who would feel sorry enough for me to join me at McDonalds for a cheeseburger.

It would seem that this Tinder would increase the chances of success without the pain. I do wonder though, what it would be like to be on this site for like a year and never get a match. Talk about destroying your self esteem! It got me to thinking that Tinder users ought to utilize the act of the sympathy swipe for exceptionally ugly people like me. Everybody deserves a right swipe every now and then.

Mom on the Go

I spent a few days visiting my eighty-nine-year-old mom in Pennsylvania last week. Her walking isn't very good these days, but she still likes to be on the go. We spent last Wednesday running errands. First stop was a place called Shorty's Lunch. They are famous for their hot dogs, awesome hot dogs with chili, mustard and onion in a little old fashioned bar/diner sort of place. I took note of a few things this trip. Typically, if you go for lunch you have to wait for a place to sit. We didn't arrive until about 1:30 so the rush had slowed a bit and we were able to immediately find an open table. The server arrived twenty-two seconds after my butt hit the chair. She took our food and drink orders (no menu required). She was back with the drinks in thirty-seven seconds, four chili dogs (two for me and two for Mom) twenty-three seconds after that. Finally, another seventeen seconds passed before she plopped two orders of French fries with brown gravy on our table. I'd like to see these fast food giants do that!

Our bellies filled, we headed out to the newspaper office. Mom wanted to purchase display memoriam ads for my father and my grandparents, in the paper, for Christmas. She sent me to scout out the premises for wheelchair access. I went inside to ask. They had no wheelchair access. I thought that all businesses were required to do that anymore. Their only access was through a revolving door and then up some stairs. Oh well, this left me to be the messenger boy between Mom and the guy inside at the counter. She drew out a little map of how each ad was to be designed, where the pictures were to go, the exact wording, the column inch size. I fear there may be hell to pay if the newspaper guy and I screw this up!

Having completed the work at the paper, our next stop was the mall for Christmas shopping. She knew exactly what she was looking for. She had spotted it in a catalog, but they wanted to charge her for shipping. How dare they! I threw her in the wheelchair and we made our way past the various stores until we finally located the one she was hunting. It was a different company from the ones who sent her the catalog and she was not happy that they didn't offer the exact same stuff! So, we had to start from scratch and look at every single item they sold so that she could feel satisfied that she had made the best selection for her gifts. Is this a woman thing or what? A man can look for two minutes and say "That'll do" and be out the door. A woman has to see them ALL, and then she usually chooses the first one she saw.

Okay Mom, my belly is full. I have gotten my exercise. It's past my nap time … what? WalMart! In December? Oh please God help me!

Yes, that's right, next stop, WalMart to pick up a "few things" she needed. When we arrived in the parking lot, she pulled her blue and white handicap placard that she bought from some guy who was selling them out of his trunk for cheap. She had me pull down front into the handicapped zone. I was then ordered to go inside and get one of those powered mart carts. Uh, all of them appeared to be occupied. However, the thought of returning to the car without one placed great fear in my body. Now, I don't know exactly how that one old lady happened to fall out of her Mart Cart over behind those clothing racks, but she seemed like she could crawl pretty fast, and oh what foul language came out of her mouth! The important thing is that I "found" Mom a mart cart.

I drove it outside where she was impatiently waiting. I helped her out of her seat and into the cart chair. I turned to lock the doors. I turned back around and BAM, she was gone like a flash! She was reaching underneath the cart making some mechanical adjustments. I never knew those carts had a turbocharged mode! Away she went, hair pinned back by the wind, people diving for cover!

She had informed me in the car that I was to go on the hunt of two items, potting soil and shelf brackets. She would be in the grocery area. Being a good son, I did as I was told and went foraging for potting soil, in December, in WalMart. Um, Mom, people do not use potting soil in December. Of course I couldn't dare tell her that. Instead, I snuck back into the back areas of the warehouse and found a small bag hidden under the racking. The shelf brackets were easier. She was gonna be so proud! I scurried along over to the grocery end of the store. Up and down the aisles I went, back and forth, all around. Mom was nowhere to be found. I looked and looked. She had disappeared. I expanded my search area, growing tired from all of the miles under my feet. Then I started to notice a path of destruction. Merchandise strewn, shoppers with a look of horror on their faces and a trail of general pandemonium. I followed it and it led me straight to Mom. Where did I finally find her? Way down at the far end of the store in Christmas decorations! "Oh, I needed a couple little fake pine trees for some baskets I am putting on that shelf you are hanging for me."

From there we finally made it out of the store. Nobody had any serious physical injuries although a few may require treatment for PTSD. Away we went, headed for home with all of our goodies in tow. I was in need of a nerve pill and a nap.

Mom? Well, all she had to say was "I am glad we got to go today. That was fun."

Pamela

"Have you ever been married?" I asked.

"No," replied Pamela. "I never married because I wouldn't tolerate abuse. Mental, physical, emotional-none of that. I would like to get married someday, but it has to be the right fit."

"What would be the right fit?" I continued.

"A companion. Somebody I can depend on. Somebody who can think outside the box and hold an intelligent conversation. He needs to have a sense of humor and to be able to just be himself. I am always just myself. I really don't do makeup or nails and hair. I am just me," she offered.

"What else?"

"He needs to have a 401k (laughs)! He needs to be active in church. I hate when I see a couple that isn't really a couple because the woman is at church and the man is somewhere else. That to me is not a companion. And he needs to have a good relationship with his mother. If he does not have a good relationship with his mother, then he probably doesn't know how to treat a woman. I have had friends who were in bad relationships and I have even spoken to them about the fact that the man was not good to his mother. It happens too often."

Pamela went on to say that she wants someone with similar goals and beliefs. Her longest relationship lasted several years on and off. She said the issue that always got in the way was religion. He was a Jehovah's Witness and she was Pentecostal. They never went to each other's church and that was an important division between them. Neither of them wanted to give up their church.

"Have you dated at all in recent times?"

"Not much." she replied. "There was this one guy who was divorced. A friend fixed me up with him (laughs). He kept saying 'I am looking for a wife'. He asked me all kinds of questions. I felt like I was applying for a job and wondered if I should ask him if there was an application I needed to fill out for this wife position. He seemed like a nice guy, but he was way overboard on this marriage mission."

"You mentioned church. Tell me more about your beliefs."

"I am Pentecostal COGIC. That's Church of God in Christ. I was raised in this denomination. I have attended other churches, Baptist for one. But, I feel more at home in my own church. I am active and involved in things there," she said. "We typically fast on Tuesdays and Fridays from midnight 'til 3:00pm. There are also two and three day fasts you can do. No food or water for three days. You are just supposed to meditate and read the Bible and be in Christ. It's not something you advertise. I don't like go to work and say 'Hey, I am fasting!' It is a personal thing. It would be important if I marry, for my husband to share in my beliefs. My mom used to have to drag me to church. She told me last year that she couldn't believe that I actually like to go to church now!"

She also talked about a few of the other things that her church adheres to such as no drinking, which I believe is common in many denominational beliefs. But the one that was interestingly different was that they only listen to Gospel music. Whether in church or in daily life, only Gospel music is played.

The best thing was that Pamela talked about how she is now comfortable with herself and if she never finds that companion, she is perfectly okay with being alone.

"I made it this far. I don't need someone to complete me," she said.

She has her faith and she has a good life. There are things that she looks forward to doing in her future and she has hopes and dreams. Pamela currently has gathered supplies to create memory books of the kids in the family for her siblings.

"I just need more space!" she professed. "When I was younger, I lived paycheck to paycheck, now I hope to be able to do more traveling."

Really, Pamela's only concern with growing older alone is who will be there to take care of her should she ever need it. This has been on her mind because just last year she cared for her own mother until she passed away from cancer. But Pamela has gone back to school and is on track to start a new career adventure in just a few more years. I would bet that there will even be some God fearing, handsome and caring man with a big 401k in her future. New horizons are opening up everywhere and she is going to be just fine.

Never Too Old

Being fifty-two and active is much different than when I would be active at twenty-two. First of all, at twenty-two it was not a conscious effort. If I wanted to be active, great. If I wanted to lie around and be lazy all day, great. My body didn't seem to care one way or the other. Now, if I lie around being lazy all day, I reach a point where I can hardly move! On the other hand, to do vigorous activity, it is now in my best interest to warm up first. Once I warm up, I can go hard for a long time. My reflexes may not be quite as quick, but my strength, I believe, is better. The big difference now comes after I am finished with an activity. Nowadays, I hurt in places on my body that I didn't even know existed at twenty-two. It doesn't stop me. I am still right back out there the next day acting like I am a kid again. I have no intention of just giving in to this whole aging thing. I will continue to do everything that I always have done for as long as I possibly can. My vertical may be six inches on the basketball court and my golf backswing may only go half way, but I will not stop.

I know that there may come a day when I will not be capable of doing certain things, but I will not let that bother me now. As far as I can tell, I only get one life. I intend to live it. I may suffer through a few more aches and pains at times, but I will earn every single one of them and suffer through them with a smile. I never want to think that I am too old to do anything.

Purgatory

"A place of suffering inhabited by the souls of sinners who are expiating their sins before going to heaven." That is the Google definition of Purgatory. I know that certain religious groups believe in such a place and yet others claim that no such place exists. Well, I am here to tell you that Purgatory does indeed exist! I have seen it with my own eyes! And there are people there too! And it is indeed a place of great suffering! There is a sign along Highway 37 pointing the way! Turn here to go to Purgatory! Purgatory Golf Club! Suddenly life has new meaning! For many of us, playing golf is indeed a form of suffering! Also, it is true that many sinners play golf and if you are not a sinner before your round, you will certainly commit several sins before the round is over!

Taking the Lord's name in vain is a big one when playing golf. You hit that beautiful shot that takes off straight for 175 yards then inexplicably makes a hard left turn into the woods. That will make a sinner out of most men!

"Thou shalt not kill" is another biggie. You hit a perfect wedge from 100 yards and your ball is intercepted by a Canadian goose flying through your airspace, causing your ball to drop 25 yards short of the green. If your ball didn't kill the goose, your hurled pitching wedge may do the trick.

"Thou shalt not steal" is a third sin. You hit a line drive that runs a bit too far and ends up rolling into a lake. You get up to the pond and find someone else's ball laying just short of the water. "Yep , that's mine! Titleist 3 right over here! Yours must have gone in the lake Charlie!" I guess that is bearing false witness too!

"Thou shalt not covet thy neighbor's possessions." Just let your neighbor show up at the course with a brand new set of Ping Anser Woods and you will see much coveting going on!

A round of golf is also a cleansing experience. It is a time and place to take your mind away from your worldly troubles for a while. So maybe Purgatory is a golf club in Indiana and maybe it is also a good place to stop on your way to Heaven.

Gender Reveal

I just saw a post on Facebook tonight that had pictures from a "gender reveal" party. Maybe I am just out of the loop, but who the heck throws one of these? I have never heard of such a thing! I mean, really, it's either a boy or a girl right? Do we really need a party for this? I asked a friend in the know and she said that they have a cake that is either pink or blue inside and that's how you know. Now, it seems to me that this is a bit over the top. Couldn't you just do a group text or a Facebook post regarding the sex of the baby? Lord knows we are all already too fat and don't need more cake! Besides, just wait a few months and the gender will be quite apparent. It will reveal itself, so to speak. Now, I get the whole idea that the mom and dad may want to know in advance, so that they know which color to paint the nursery. It is not a necessity, but I can understand why people feel the urge to know. As for me, I would prefer it to be a surprise, but I am probably just old school.

I guess I can see some other uses for this concept. Maybe Maury could bring out a cake after the DNA testing and let the woman cut into it to find a picture of who is the real baby daddy.

Then they could all throw cake at one another if they didn't like the answer. Perhaps, the reveal cake could also be used by a secret admirer. Send an anonymous bouquet of flowers followed by a cake with your picture hidden in the middle. She is much more likely to say yes on a full stomach.

✳✳✳

It is Sunday, September 7th. It is around 5:30pm and it is 74 degrees outside and sunny with low humidity. I played racquetball this morning against my friend, Kasim. I won three games to one. I then went and had Jambalaya for lunch. Beginning at 1:00pm, week one of NFL football nirvana began on TV. Could a day be more perfect? What more could a man ask for?

Only One

If you only had one bowl from which to eat and you knew that you could never get another one, would you take good care of that bowl, clean it thoroughly after each use, handle it with care, keep it safe, and use it wisely?

If you had only one pair of shoes and knew you could never get another, would you take good care of those shoes, keep them clean, use them with care, store them in a dry place, and be thankful to have them?

What if you only had one body and could never get another? Would you keep it clean and properly nourished, keep it fit, keep it in top running condition? Would you be thankful and use it with care?

But wait, you do only have one body. Do you treat it the same way you would treat that single bowl or single pair of shoes? Do you nourish it only with what is good for it? Do you keep it in top condition? Are you thankful to have it since it is the only one you can inhabit? It is the only earthly home you will ever know. Do you cherish it as such?

What about your life? As far as we know, you only get one of those too! Do you take good care of it and cherish it? Are you thankful for it every single day? Do you keep it safe and use it wisely?

☝

Ralph

Hi, my name is Ralph, well at least I thought so until today. I live in a storm drain near where all of those big, noisy machines that go fast, then slow down; the ones with the humans inside. They call it an Interstate exit ramp. I haven't always lived there, but I have been there for quite some time now, so long that I cannot even remember where I lived before. It's not easy. My home is kinda stinky, but it is safe, well, except for those little biting bugs, but otherwise, I feel safe there. I get my food from over behind those big buildings in the distance, at night, when nobody is looking. I get by. Well, that was until today.

Today started out fairly normal. Sunshine, grasshoppers, crickets, lots of those big fast machines, like always. But, halfway through my day, everything sort of went crazy. I was just hanging out at the entrance to my storm drain when a human came walking up. She looked okay and made my grass wiggle with her finger, so I decided to come out and offer to let her smell my butt. Just about then, she snatched my up and held me really tight! She carried me while walking hurriedly toward one of those big, fast machines. As we approached, the machine opened its mouth really wide and spit out another, smaller human. They both began to make funny noises directed at me. I was confused. Soon, the machine swallowed all three of us whole. Inside, was yet another, big, ugly human as well. That machine must have been very hungry. As soon as its mouth was closed, the machine took off and raced away at incredible speeds. It wasn't but a few minutes later that the machine must have gotten sick because it suddenly stopped and spit all four of us out! I bet those humans don't taste very good.

For me, things started to go downhill fast from there. The humans took me inside a building where there were even more humans who seemed to be quite happy to see me. The trouble is that they seemed a bit too happy! I felt so violated as they poked and prodded and squeezed even my most personal possessions! Then, the first three humans just left me there to be subjected to some sort of water torture! I am telling you, it was the most horrible thing a cat could ever endure! I thought I was a goner!

Strangely enough they stuck me in a cardboard box and soon the first three humans had returned again! I was so confused by this point. At least these three seemed nice. We were swallowed by the machine again, and yet again, it got sick and spit us out. It is now dark. I have been given a private room, lots of food, a portable bathroom, and a soft blanket to nap upon. I am not sure what exactly is happening, but these humans seem nice enough. Maybe I should retain them as my servants. Except, they keep calling me Pi. Oh well, just keep the kibble and tuna coming!

Goodbye Mom

We are all here today because someone we care about has passed away. She was mom to me, grandma to others, great grandma, aunt, coworker, friend. She carried many titles in life. Lunch lady, cake lady, crazy old lady behind the wheel … many titles. We are also most likely reflecting a bit on our own mortality today. For each one of us, there will come a day when people will gather to mourn our passing. And I believe that each and every one of us would be honored to be remembered as fondly as my mom, Betty Jean Chambers Hewitt.

She was a woman with a caring and genuine heart. I have also heard her referred to countless times as the strongest woman most of us have ever known. I have never forgotten something she once told me many years ago. She said, "You know, there is nothing I can't do if someone just shows me how." That's simple statement stuck with me. I saw her live this statement time and time again. Not only was she a great cook and the cake lady, she was an Avon lady, she worked at the nursing home, she was a census taker many times over, she last worked the census in 2010… She also worked in the butcher shop, she was an election worker, a ladies auxiliary volunteer, she cleaned the houses of elderly shut-ins, tended fifty or sixty head of cattle and she took care of a family. How do I know all of these things? Because she dragged me and my brother along to each and every one of these adventures. We also raised gardens, cared for livestock, picked berries, dug a good 50 bushel of taters most years, snapped beans, shelled peas, canned fruit and froze corn all summer for the coming winters....we were a busy bunch! We were far from rich, but through hard work and perseverance nobody ever went hungry or was cold or felt unwanted.

I have just told you about a few of my mother's good qualities. One other major part of what made her who she was her love of animals. She sometimes told the story of how she would run outside as a child when her mother was selecting a chicken for Sunday dinner to make sure none of her favorites were taken. She said it was difficult to eat when you knew that Charlie, the chicken you had named and loved, was now the main course. Many of you knew her as the cat lady. My mother would take care of any cat that needed a home. We fed them and medicated them and housed them...Charles and I were the only children in the neighborhood with a cat house in our yard. Mom also had a soft spot for dogs. We think she may have fed a few of them to death, but they died fat and happy. The other animal my mother loved was the turtle. Many times I can recall her slamming on the brakes and jumping out to snatch up a turtle that was crossing the road. She would deliver it somewhere to a safe patch of grass and send it on its way. There was no living thing for which she didn't show compassion and kindness.

Wouldn't we all be happy to be remembered for so many positive ways in which we made a difference? My mom is a shining example of a life well lived. Ninety+ years of making the world a better place because she was in it. So, while this is indeed a sad occasion, let it also be a celebration of a very successful journey down life's road and a lesson to us all.

The Storm

I just sat on my front porch and watched a storm roll in. It was a dandy, gusty winds and heavy rain, rumbling thunder. When I was a country kid, this was a regular event in summertime. With no air conditioning, you would go outside and embrace those cool breezes coming in off of the rain. I learned a good bit about how weather works from those porch sessions. I would watch the churning clouds, the flashes of lightning, count the seconds till the accompanying thunder, listen to the rain slapping against the metal porch roof.

What prompted me to sit outside today was a trip to the mailbox. Actually, it was my normal trip to the mailbox and then to the garbage can to deposit the mail. Publishers Clearing House still hasn't sent me my prizes, but that's another story. You see, I went to the mailbox and I could see it was clouding up a bit. I didn't need to go back inside and check The Weather Channel. The birds were telling me everything I needed to know. A warm day in July and there was dead silence, an eerie silence. That's always the sign that a good storm is imminent. The animals know. They have some extra sensory ability that we humans lack. Maybe it's just better hearing or something, I don't know. I still remember my old dog, Shorty, when I was a kid. He would start pacing back and forth about two hours before a storm. He just knew.

Today's storm was fast moving and lasted all of twenty minutes. I took it all in, the cooling breezes, the misty outflow from the torrential rains. I even counted the seconds between the thunder and lightning. I felt renewed and refreshed as once again I felt like a ten-year-old kid on the porch with my mom, my dad and my grandpa taking in a summer storm.

Growing Pains

For a fifty-two-year-old, I am quite active. I play golf, racquetball, tennis, go cycling, walking and running, play basketball, etc. ... I love to be moving. Because of these things, I am in decent shape comparatively. My upper body is not overly strong, but my legs have been powerful for many years, mainly due to my cycling. I love to ride hills and ride fast. My legs are never sore from exercise unlike my wimpy arms, which ache regularly. There are even a couple leg machines at the gym that I can do on max weight, which is unusual because I am not of particularly muscular build. The problem, however, that I am painfully aware of at this moment, has to do with muscle memory. If you do the same thing enough, your body gets used to that activity and breezes right through it. No pain, no stress. But, do something out of the ordinary and your body may not respond so easily.

For me, this became all to clear about three days ago when I did a new and seemingly benign ten minute workout. I didn't even break a sweat. Compared to a two hour racquetball match or a twenty-five mile bike ride, this workout was chump change; at least until I attempted to crawl out of bed the next morning! My quadriceps were so sore and are still sore now, three days later! I obviously need more variety in my workouts! And perhaps a Colts cheerleader or two to come by and give me a daily massage.

Window Tinting

Window tinting on cars should be outlawed! It interferes with my traffic light gawking. I know that I am not the only one who likes to look at other people at a stop light or in a good traffic jam. It's entertaining. I see people eating, doing makeup, surfin' the internet, singing. The singing is one of my favorites. People get into their own little world, close their eyes and do this seated dancing thing. Some of them have moves I have never seen before! When you put tinted windows on these cars, it deprives me of my entertainment.

As a response to this epidemic, I have started vigorously smiling and waving at cars beside me that have tinted windows. I even mix in a few mouthed words. It's a fun game! I win if I can get them to roll down the window. I just don't think it's fair that they can see out and we can't see in. I think we should legislate this matter and ban window tinting. Be honest. When you see a limo, don't you want to know who is inside there? Most of the people in a limo wouldn't matter a hill of beans to me, but if it happened to be Rachel McAdams in there, I would want to know! The window tinting would just prevent that instant connection that I know she would feel for me! Fate would be interrupted by that damned tinting! So, let's join forces and eradicate this problem once and for all in a bipartisan effort. We need a slogan, something that rhymes with tint and gets the message out that this crap has got to go! My future with Rachel may be riding on this!

The Life Lottery

I am sure that, if you are like most people, you have daydreamed a time or two about all of the wonderful things you would do if you won the lottery. Whether your dreams involve endless travel or charity work or retirement or buying a big ranch and disappearing from society, we each have our own perfect scenario in our minds. I don't think many of us would ever complain, "Well, I just spent $30 million dollars and I still have another $220 million to go!" or "Oh, I wish they hadn't sent me so much money!" Sounds kinda silly doesn't it? You would probably feel lucky and blessed to have been the "chosen one" out of countless millions to be in this situation, right?

Well, guess what? You have already won the lottery! You have been a grand prize winner of something so valuable even money cannot buy! You have won the life lottery! The odds of you being alive right now are infinitesimal. Over the past few hundred years alone, over a million people had to fall in love for you to ever have any chance of standing here today. You don't believe me? Well, let's do a little math lesson. You had two parents, right? And to make the math simple, let's say that your parents were 30-years-old when you were born and your grandparents were 30 when your parents were born, etc... So, on the day of your birth, you had two parents, go back 30 years and your two parents were brought into this world by four grandparents. 30 years before that, there were eight great grand parents celebrating a new baby, then continuing in 30 year jumps, there were sixteen, then thirty-two, then sixty-four then one hundred twenty-eight and that day, if my calculations are right, was only somewhere in the late 1700s or early 1800s depending on your age. So, let's average that out at 1800. In 1800, there were 128 people who had to do all of the right things for you to be here today.

Let's go a bit deeper. So, at thirty years per generation, that would make ten generations in three hundred years, right? We have already determined that in 1800 there were 128 future pieces of you walking around. If we go back another ten generations to 1500, I wonder what that number might be? Starting at 128...256, 512, 1024, 2048, 4096, 8192....omg I need a calculator... 16384, 32768, 65536, 131072. That's ten generations. At that point, there were 131072 pieces of you out there... One final step, those 131,000+ people had 262,000 parents, 524,000 grandparents, and 1,048,000 great grandparents. That would take us back to the year 1400 approximately. Now, I realize that many people had their babies before age thirty, so this is a highly conservative estimate.

I was curious, so I looked up the world population in the year 1400. It was estimated to be around 400 million people. This means that one out of every 400 people on the entire planet at that time was carrying around a piece of what would eventually become you! If just one of that million had made a wrong turn and become dinner for a lion or fallen off a cliff or gotten into a sword fight with the wrong person, you wouldn't be here!

Now, I do realize that great, great, great, great, great, great, great, great, great grandpa might not have been faithful and that somewhere along the line your family tree might have some oddly connected branches which make your great aunt also your third cousin, but the general math is difficult to contest. You are already incredibly lucky.

So, here you sit with this grand prize in the life lottery! Are you enjoying your prize or squandering it, wasting it by complaining, being negative about it, wishing away your days or are you enjoying every second, every moment, basking in the great fortune of this incredible gift? Just like the lottery money, the Life Lottery Grand Prize will run out. When it does, will you be sitting there wondering where it all went? Or will you be smiling from ear to ear and proclaiming, "Man! What a ride!"

Giving

I just love people-watching. It is a cold February evening. Temperature is in the twenties, not horrible for this time of year, but cold. I am sitting in a large strip mall parking lot. This place has a mixture of businesses, a Goodwill Store, an Asian grocery, a country and western nightclub, a boating accessory store, a weight loss place, a cell phone place, a musical instrument store, a buffet restaurant, a beauty supply place, a Japanese steakhouse, and a place to get your hair done ... Oh wait, I also see one place that is a beauty college and a place that says it makes your feet euphoric, and then there is one called the Learning Shop. It makes no mention of what you might be able to learn there, but it's there if you have been looking for it. Oops, just spotted two more ... a sub shop and a nutritional supplement place. I drive through this parking lot on a regular basis and had no idea over half of these places even existed here. It is as if I have been numbed by an over abundance of choices in the area. This is just one plaza among countless ones nearby.

People like me, who live in suburbia, have way too much of everything to choose from, grocery stores, places to eat, fitness clubs, banks, clothing stores, just everything. Even doctors and hospitals are a dime a dozen. From my house, in fifteen minutes, give or take, I could arrive at the emergency room of seven hospitals that I can think of off the top of my head. I live within five minutes of six major grocery stores, hundreds of doctor's offices. I can't even count the places to eat, and probably five gyms. There are banks on every corner. It's just crazy.

Matter of fact, let me talk about the bank for a moment. My personal bank has two locations within five minutes of my house. One of them is open 'til 7:00 weeknights and 6:00 on Saturdays. Then, a couple of years ago, when I was dating Wendy, we had a need to open a joint checking account, so we went to this other bank that was new to town. Wendy had chosen it, for whatever reason and I really didn't care one way or the other. When Wendy and I parted company, I just kept an account open there. So, altogether, I have been banking there for probably two years or a bit more. I have never seen another customer in that bank, ever! When I go in, the teller is sitting there watching television, just hanging out. Compare that to my original bank which always seems to be bustling with activity. It's just weird. I am not sure how bank number two exists on my hundred dollars I keep in there and I believe that Wendy still probably has an account there, but she is no richer than I am. I have no clue how they could stay in business like that.

So, anyhow, where was I? In suburbia you have too much of everything. I have also lived many years of my life in the country, where you exist just fine with almost nothing within fifteen minutes or even thirty minutes. Heck, in Tennessee, I had to drive a good fifteen or twenty just to reach a gas station. In Pennsylvania, it was a solid half an hour, if you were lucky, to get to the most basic hospital emergency room, a full sized grocery store was even a bit further. Now, this is all in what we call the civilized world. I did some Googling and found an interview on voice of America news that had been conducted with a doctor at a rural hospital in South Africa, which is far from being the poorest country there. He said that often, in order to get an ambulance available to transfer a very sick patient to a better-equipped facility, required a wait of ten to twelve hours. Can you even imagine? That's for a necessity! I can't even begin to guess how far they must travel for many of the other conveniences we take for granted every day.

I know that many people do not like to think about or seriously talk about such things, but it's a sad reality. Every major religion speaks of helping those in need. In the Bible, Matthew 5:42 says "Give to the one who begs from you," Proverbs 28:27 says "Whoever gives to the poor will not want, but he who hides his eyes will get many a curse." Also, people with zero religious affiliation also frequently believe in charity. Yet, almost all of us turn a blind eye. We are wasteful and greedy and are perfectly okay with suffering, as long as it is not in our own backyard. I have been as guilty as the next person, but I am working toward changing my way of doing things. If I am lucky, perhaps I can inspire others as well.

I Like Dreaming

I love dreams! My own mind is so capable of creating riveting, entertaining, interactive theater without rehearsals or scripts or a $100 million budget. I just awoke from one of those masterpieces and decided that I need to tell you about it before I forget.

You see, I was staying at some apartment building and there was a greenway running by it. I decided that Curt and I should take a bike ride together. When I went outside, that cute girl that used to work at my bank was patrolling. She stopped me and asked if I had had my bike inspected. I said no, that it was a brand new bike and worked just fine. I didn't know that it needed to be inspected. She assured me that all bicycles that used the greenway needed to be inspected. I was kinda in a hurry to catch up with Curt. I asked her where I could get it inspected. She told me that she had forgotten then name of the street, but if I followed her, she would show me. Far be it from me to not follow a pretty girl, so I said okay. She hopped in her car and took off just flying down the road! I peddled as fast as I could, but I just could not keep up!

Fortunately, it was not long before I noticed the place where my mom lives. I went in to ask her what she knew. She said that she believed that the bicycle inspection place was in Washington, about 25 miles away. She wasn't sure, but she thought that my brother had been there recently. We hopped in her car and proceeded to go find my brother. The road we were driving on was covered in wet grass. It was slippery and we did some fish tailing, but I was in a hurry and besides, it was kind of fun.

When we located my brother, he was sitting in a yard playing checkers with the boy who used to live up the road a mile or so from my house. I explained my dilemma and he acknowledged that he had indeed been to the bicycle inspection place and that it was in Waynesburg, on the south side of town on a street called either Oak Tree Road or Moxie Road, he couldn't remember for sure. I asked him to just give me directions. He couldn't remember how to get there. He told me to just go drive around until I found it. So, that's what Mom and I did.

As we headed back toward town, we drove through Rogersville. It was a Saturday, along about 6:00pm or so, and there were a few hundred people out walking around on the main drag. Considering that the total town population is about 250 people, whatever was going on had to be very big! I didn't have time to stop and investigate even with Mom's protests because I needed to find the bicycle inspection place before it closed! Now, remember, I was now in a car and my bike was back where my mom lives and Curt had already left, riding down the greenway, but none of that mattered at this moment. You see, I hate to fail and I was determined to get my bike inspected, no matter what!

Just about then, a garbage truck started making noise outside and I woke up! Damned garbage truck! Now I will never find the bicycle inspection place and Curt will be wondering what happened to me and the cute girl from my bank will think I abandoned her and … I know! I think I should go back to bed and see if I can finish my dream! After all it's rainy and cold outside and so I would much rather just hide under the covers and get my bicycle inspected then go out there in the real world today.

Unflat Tire

A friend of mine mentioned buying new tires today and it reminded me of a recent experience. I swear these things never happen to other people! No, really, even the mechanic said he had never seen such a thing. The whole incident started innocently enough. My car kept telling me it was time for an oil change. So, I took it to a place that only does tires and oil. I always seems if you take it anywhere that does much engine work, they will find something else you need done too, like a transmission overhaul or a new exhaust system. So, anyway, this place, as part of your oil change checks levels of all fluids, tire pressure, lights, wipers, silly stuff. The old guy who was doing my service came into the waiting room after I had been there about forty-five minutes. He was scratching his head. He gestured for me to come with him to the shop. Uh, okay?

He said, "I have never seen something like this in my life." He then showed me that he had completely removed the pressure valve from my tire, and yet he could not get any air into or out of it, none.

"I don't know if there is any air in your tire or not!" he continued. "Being this type of tire it may just be running on the sidewalls. It could have been this way for months." So, this guy was telling me that I had a flat tire for months driving 80mph down the interstate and I didn't even know it? So, where's the problem right? Why go fixing things that are working? But, he insisted he needed to take the tire off the rim and see what was going on. When he opened the tire, he found about a gallon of water inside and the valve was rusted shut. He then decided that I needed a new tire.

Now, wait a minute! I drove in here just fine for an oil change. Now, you tell me I need a new tire to drive back home. He said he had never seen anything like it! I agreed, although I think we were talking about two different things. But he had the upper hand. My car was four feet in the air wearing three wheels. The mechanic had the keys and my credit card number. So not fair! I had big plans for that money! Now he was shoving it into his own pocket because he wouldn't let me drive around on a perfectly good flat tire! Next time I need an oil change, I am gonna make the kids do it!

Jiffy Brake

I had that familiar grinding sound of a worn brake pad appear on the front of my car yesterday. It's nineteen degrees for a high today with snow and ice and my garage is full of all of the stuff that my children have left behind when they moved to college. So, this afternoon, I ventured out into the frozen tundra known as my driveway and completed the world's fastest brake job in approximately fifteen minutes using only a tire iron, a jack, a screwdriver, duct tape and a socket wrench, and I only had two bolts and some little squiggly wire thingy left over when I was finished! I am such a mechanic! It has me thinking that I should go over to the Indy Speedway and look into openings on a pit crew.

www.ingramcontent.com/pod-product-compliance
Lightning Source LLC
Chambersburg PA
CBHW031957040426
42448CB00006B/389